COMPREHENSIVE ASSURANCE & SYSTEMS TOOL

An Integrated Practice Set

FRANK A. BUCKLESS

North Carolina State University

LAURA R. INGRAHAM

San Jose State University

J. GREGORY JENKINS

North Carolina State University

Computerized AIS Module

PEARSON

Prentice Hall

Upper Saddle River, New Jersey

Library of Congress Cataloging-in-Publication information is available.

Acquisitions Editor: Bill Larkin
Editor-in-Chief: Jeff Shelstad
Assistant Editor: Sam Goffinet
Editorial Assistant: Jane Avery
Marketing Manager: Beth Toland
Marketing Assistant: Patrick Danzuso
Managing Editor: John Roberts
Manufacturing Buyer: Michelle Klein
Production Manager: Arnold Vila
Cover Design Manager: Jayne Conte
Cover Photo: Craig Brewer/Photodisc/Getty Images, Inc.
Printer/Binder: Courier–Bookmart

Pearson Education LTD.
Pearson Education Singapore, Pte. Ltd
Pearson Education, Canada, Ltd
Pearson Education–Japan

Pearson Education Australia PTY, Limited
Pearson Education North Asia Ltd
Pearson Educación de Mexico, S.A. de C.V.
Pearson Education Malaysia, Pte. Ltd

10 9 8 7 6 5 4 3 2 1
ISBN 0-13-046469-4

Table of Contents

Computerized AIS Module

Preface

The Comprehensive Assurance and Systems Tool (CAST) provides an integrated learning opportunity that encompasses financial statement assurance and accounting information systems. CAST uniquely exposes students to these issues at The Winery at Chateau Americana, a hypothetical company that is based on an actual domestic winery. Unlike traditional projects and assignments that may offer little or no context, students develop a rich knowledge and understanding of Chateau Americana and its industry as they provide assurance on the company's financial statements and address a variety of challenging accounting information systems issues.

CAST is comprised of three self-contained, but complementary modules:
- The *Manual AIS module* requires students to complete real-world business documents, journalize and post a variety of transactions, and prepare a year-end worksheet. This module may be completed before or during the completion of either the Accounting Information Systems module or the Assurance module. However, students are not required to complete this module before the other modules.
- The *Accounting Information Systems module* is comprised of three components: spreadsheets, general ledger software, and databases. Although self-contained, this module's value is greatest when combined with the Manual AIS module.
- The *Assurance module* provides students hands-on experience with fundamental elements of financial statement assurance. This module is comprised of components related to the client acceptance decision, understanding the business environment, understanding and testing internal controls, assessing risks and materiality, conducting substantive tests, evaluating attorney's letters, performing analytical review procedures, and determining the appropriate audit opinion. These components build upon one another and should be completed in the order in which they are presented.

CAST can be implemented in either an undergraduate or graduate setting and is ideally suited for simultaneous integration across assurance and information systems courses. In addition, each of the modules can be completed either as an in-class or an out-of-class assignment. CAST affords students the opportunity to develop and strengthen their analytical thinking, written and oral communication, problem solving, and team building skills.

We believe your students will benefit from using CAST and we encourage you to contact us with questions or suggestions about how we can improve the materials.

Frank Buckless
Laura Ingraham
Greg Jenkins

SPREADSHEET APPLICATIONS USING MICROSOFT® EXCEL 2002: The Winery at Chateau Americana

LEARNING OBJECTIVES

After completing and discussing this module, you should be able to:

- Recognize the managerial and technological issues and risks associated with designing and utilizing a spreadsheet application as the primary accounting information system
- Understand and evaluate data integrity issues associated with spreadsheet utilization
- Understand and perform data analysis techniques using spreadsheet applications
- Understand the advantages and disadvantages of various presentation formats
- Understand the advantages and disadvantages of database functions in spreadsheet applications

BACKGROUND

When Chateau Americana began operations in 1980, accounting records were maintained manually. As the winery grew, the former CFO decided it was time to computerize various aspects of the system. As an initial step, he decided to use a spreadsheet program to assist in preparing journal entries, the year-end worksheet, and the financial statements. He also wanted to be able to create a single set of financial statements that could be used to present differing amounts of information to the various users. His goal was to simplify the bookkeeping functions, while improving the accuracy and usefulness of the financial statements. He knew this could be done by reducing the amount of redundancy inherent in manual recordkeeping. If the data was entered once and was verified at that time, this data could then be transmitted to other spreadsheets without the risk of incurring clerical errors that might appear upon re-entering the same data. He, therefore, had created various spreadsheets for Chateau Americana that would assist in these goals.

Assume that you had been asked to create these spreadsheets for Chateau Americana, given the current year end data. The following exercises were written assuming that you would be working in *Microsoft® Excel 2002*. If this is not the case, some minor adjustments may need to be made to the instructions. In addition, a general tutorial consisting of basic information has been provided for novice Excel users at the end of the exercises. If you are not a novice user, you may skip that section entirely. Finally, tutorials follow many of the sections, providing hints and additional explanations for some of the more advanced Excel skill requirements. The symbol ⌘ denotes areas for which additional tutorial explanation is provided.

As with any other computer file, it is important to **save your work often** and to **back it up frequently** to another storage medium.

Download and save the Excel file entitled "CA_excel.xls" from the CAST web site (your instructor will provide you with the URL for this web site). This workbook contains several worksheets that will be necessary for the completion of the various exercises contained in the Spreadsheet assignment.

PROTECTING THE DATA

Open the **CA_excel** file you have downloaded. This file contains several worksheets including a blank year-end worksheet similar to the one you may have completed in the Manual AIS Module of *CAST* entitled **Y-E Worksheet**. Examine the set-up of the year-end worksheet, familiarizing yourself with the ways in which the creation of formulas in Excel can be used to minimize the amount of data input.

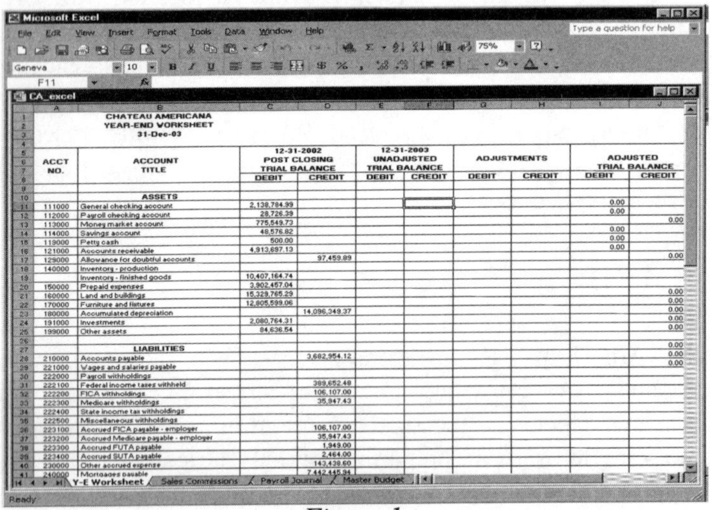

CHATEAU AMERICANA
YEAR-END WORKSHEET
31-Dec-03

ACCT NO.	ACCOUNT TITLE	12-31-2002 POST CLOSING TRIAL BALANCE DEBIT	CREDIT	12-31-2003 UNADJUSTED TRIAL BALANCE DEBIT	CREDIT	ADJUSTMENTS DEBIT	CREDIT	ADJUSTED TRIAL BALANCE DEBIT	CREDIT
	ASSETS								
111000	General checking account	2,138,784.99						0.00	
112000	Payroll checking account	28,726.39						0.00	
113000	Money market account	775,549.73							0.00
114000	Savings account	48,576.82						0.00	
119000	Petty cash	500.00						0.00	
121000	Accounts receivable	4,913,697.13						0.00	
129000	Allowance for doubtful accounts		97,459.89						0.00
140000	Inventory - production								
	Inventory - finished goods	10,407,164.74							
150000	Prepaid expenses	3,902,457.04							
160000	Land and buildings	15,329,765.29							0.00
170000	Furniture and fixtures	12,805,599.06							0.00
180000	Accumulated depreciation		14,096,349.37						0.00
191000	Investments	2,080,764.31							0.00
199000	Other assets	84,636.54							0.00
	LIABILITIES								0.00
210000	Accounts payable		3,682,954.12						0.00
221000	Wages and salaries payable								0.00
222000	Payroll withholdings								
222100	Federal income taxes withheld		389,652.48						
222200	FICA withholdings		106,107.00						
222300	Medicare withholdings		35,947.43						
222400	State income tax withholdings								
222500	Miscellaneous withholdings								
223100	Accrued FICA payable - employer		106,107.00						
223200	Accrued Medicare payable - employer		35,947.43						
223300	Accrued FUTA payable		1,949.00						
223400	Accrued SUTA payable		2,464.00						
230000	Other accrued expense		143,438.60						
240000	Mortgages payable		7,442,445.94						

Figure 1

Requirements

1. Open the **CA_excel** file and enter on the **Y-E Worksheet**, the data for the 12-31-03 Unadjusted Trial Balance and the 12-31-03 Adjustments columns, allowing the formulas contained in the spreadsheet to calculate the totals and carry the figures from one column of the spreadsheet to the next (i.e., from those columns to the Adjusted Trial Balance, Balance Sheet, and Income Statement columns). The data for completion of this worksheet are available on the CAST web site.

2. Review the worksheet to be sure that your column totals are accurate and that you have entered the correct data for each account.

3. Once you have made certain that the embedded formulas are being calculated correctly, you should lock the cells that contain them so that no one can change the formulas at a later date. To do this, highlight cells **I9** through **N91** and then lock them ⌘.

4. Now protect ⌘ the locked cells.

5. Verify that the cells have been locked properly by attempting to alter any of the formulas contained in columns I through N.

> **Protecting the Data Tutorial**
> Highlight the cells to be locked. Click on **Format > Cells > Protection**. Click on the "Locked" box and click on "OK". Once you have locked all of the desired cells, click on **Tools > Protection > Protect Sheet**. The Protect Sheet pop-up window will appear with the "Protect worksheet and contents of locked cells" box checked. Enter a password that will enable you to unlock the cells at a later date, if necessary. You will then be prompted to confirm the password by reentering it. **NOTE:** If you do not enter a password, any user can unprotect the worksheet.

FORMULA AUDITING

The spreadsheet is now ready to be used for the creation of the financial statements and manipulation of the data for various managerial tasks. Before you begin, however, it is important to recognize that, despite the fact that you will be using a computer to deal with many of the clerical tasks previously done manually, the computer can do so accurately only insofar as the formulas are entered correctly. Statistics show that the number of errors on computer worksheets exceeds 25%. Some of the more common errors are:

# NAME?	Occurs when Excel cannot evaluate a defined name used in the formula because the name may never have existed, may be misspelled, or may have been inadvertently deleted.
# N/A	Dependent upon the formula. For example, it may mean that no value was available in a vlookup function.
#REF!	Indicates a problem with a cell reference due, perhaps, to deleting cells, rows or columns used in a formula.
# VALUE!	Typically due to trying to use a cell containing text in a calculation or entering incorrect arguments.

The **Formula Auditing** tool in Excel enables the user to audit the worksheet to find and correct many of the errors that inevitably occur.

Requirements
As you work through the following steps, you will occasionally be asked questions. Please respond to these questions in the space provided in the **Sales Commissions** worksheet.

1. Open the **CA_excel** file and click on the **Sales Commissions** worksheet. Display the **Formula Auditing** toolbar by clicking on **Tools > Formula Auditing > Show Formula Auditing Toolbar**.

Figure 2

The following table describes some of the buttons on the toolbar:

Option	Description
Error Checking	Describes the error that has occurred and allows the user to obtain help on the error, to walk through the calculation steps, to ignore the error, or to edit the error in the formula bar.
Trace Precedents	Displays a blue arrow from all cells that supply data to the selected cell.
Remove Precedent Arrows	Removes all precedent arrows for each level displayed. The button must be pushed for each level from which the data is supplied.
Trace Dependents	Displays a red arrow that is dependent upon the selected cell for data.
Remove Dependent Arrows	Removes all dependent arrows for each level displayed. The button must be pushed for each level to which the data are supplied.
Remove All Arrows	Removes all tracer arrows throughout the worksheet.
Trace Errors	Allows the user to find the source of an error by displaying a blue arrow from the source of the error to the selected cell.
New Comment	Allows the user to add comments to a cell.
Circle Invalid Data	Displays a red circle around cells that break any validation rules the user stipulates.
Clear Validation Circles	Removes all validation circles.
Show Watch Window	Displays a window that enables the user to watch what happens to a chosen cell and its formula even when the cell may be off the screen.
Evaluate Formula	Allows the user to display the result of any underlined or italicized portion of a formula.

2. Go to cell **G30**. Click on **Trace Precedents** on the **Formula Auditing** toolbar. From what cell is cell **G30** obtaining its data? (Enter your response in cell **B48**.)

3. Now click on **Remove Precedent Arrows** on the **Formula Auditing** toolbar.

4. While cell **G30** is highlighted, click on **Error Checking** on the **Formula Auditing** toolbar. Obtain two possible causes for the error by clicking on **Help on this error** and enter the two causes in cell **B49**. Close the **Error Checking** window.

5. While cell **G30** is highlighted, click on **Evaluate Formula** on the **Formula Auditing** toolbar. Next, click on **Evaluate**. Why has the error occurred? (Enter your response in cell **B50**.)

6. Examine the cells surrounding **G30** and then fix the error in cell **G30**.

7. Go to cell **F35**. Click on **Trace Precedents** on the **Formula Auditing** toolbar. What happens? (Enter your response in cell **B51**.)

8. While cell **F35** is highlighted, click on **Trace Dependents** on the **Formula Auditing** toolbar. What happens? (Enter your response in cell **B52**.)

9. While cell **F35** is highlighted, click on **Evaluate Formula** on the **Formula Auditing** toolbar. Next, click on **Evaluate** and determine why the error has occurred and then fix it. (Enter your response in cell **B53**.)

10. Check to be sure that all errors on this worksheet have been fixed.

DATA INTEGRITY

Using the **Y-E Worksheet** you can create the Statement of Income and Retained Earnings and the Balance Sheet with very little additional data entry. This is beneficial because you have already verified the accuracy of the data on the **Y-E Worksheet**. If you use this data directly, you will only need to verify the logic on the other spreadsheets you are preparing. One method by which this can be accomplished is to utilize the "=" sign to tell Excel that a particular cell is equal to the amount in another cell on another spreadsheet. Another method is to create a Name for a particular amount to be used later in a formula. You will utilize both of these methods.

The Statement of Income and Retained Earnings is to be prepared as a **single-year, multi-step income statement**. This statement is to be formatted so that it can provide differing amounts of detail to the users when viewed or printed at a later date. To do this, you will need to pay careful attention to the formatting instructions provided below. Do not attempt to enter any amounts until you are finished formatting. Then carefully read the directions in step 8 to continue with the data entry. You may find it helpful to refer to *Figure 3* as you work through the income statement instructions.

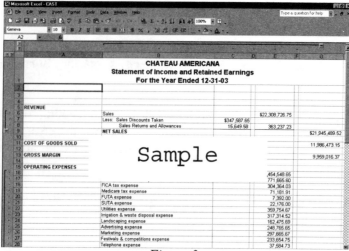

Figure 3

Requirements

1. Open the **CA_excel** file and insert a new worksheet. Format the columns for the following widths ⌘:

A	B	C	D	E	F	G
31	38	14	1	14	1	17

Column A will contain the category headings. Column B will contain the account titles. Columns C, E and G will contain amounts. The single space columns (columns D and F) are to provide a slight space between the columns containing amounts.

Set the row height for row 1 at 71 ⌘. It is not necessary to adjust the heights of the remaining rows.

2. Rename the newly inserted worksheet "**Income Statement**."

3. Column B will be used for individual revenue and expense account titles such as Sales, Wages and Salaries Expense, etc. Starting in row 6 of column B, enter the revenue and expense account titles listed on the **Y-E Worksheet**. (**HINT**: Be sure that you have copied and entered on the new worksheet all account titles needed to create the Statement of Income and Retained Earnings. The ordering and presentation of the account titles should be consistent with that commonly used on income statements, not that found on the **Y-E Worksheet**.)

4. Column A will be used for category headings. Beginning on row 5 in column A, enter the category heading "REVENUE." Enter the following headings in subsequent rows in column A: COST OF GOODS SOLD, GROSS MARGIN, OPERATING EXPENSES, INCOME FROM OPERATIONS, OTHER INCOME AND EXPENSES, INCOME (LOSS) BEFORE TAXES, FEDERAL INCOME TAX, NET

INCOME (LOSS), RETAINED EARNINGS - 12/31/2002, RETAINED EARNINGS - 12/31/2003, and EARNINGS PER SHARE.

5. Capitalize the main headings in column A using bold Arial 10. Use non-bold Arial 10 for the account titles in column B. Be sure to underline when appropriate using borders ⌘.

6. Column C should be used for amounts that must be added to arrive at subtotals. For example, the amounts for Sales Returns and Allowances and Sales Discounts should be placed in column C. These are combined to arrive at the amount that is subtracted from Sales to compute Net Sales, which is then presented in column G along with the other main category totals (see *Figure 3*).

7. Properly format your amounts for currency (i.e., with dollar signs, commas, decimal points, etc.) ⌘ where appropriate. REMEMBER: Decimal points are supposed to line up!

8. Create a heading ⌘ in cell **A1** as follows:

   Chateau Americana, Inc. (using bold Arial 14)
   Statement of Income and Retained Earnings (using bold Arial 12)
   For the Year ended 12/31/03 (using bold Arial 12)

   Center the heading across columns A through G.

9. Copy the appropriate amounts to the **Income Statement** bold worksheet by typing an "=," locating the appropriate cell on the **Y-E Worksheet (HINT:** Most of these amounts should be taken from columns M through P), and hitting **Enter.** Note, however, that Retained Earnings on the **Y-E Worksheet** has not yet been updated for the current year Net Income. Therefore, the amount in cell **N42** on the **Y-E Worksheet** represents Retained Earnings as of 12-31-02. You will have to use a formula on the **Income Statement** worksheet to calculate Retained Earnings as of 12-31-03.

10. Skip steps 11 through 13 if your instructor does not want you to calculate federal income taxes on the **Income Statement** worksheet using a nested "IF" statement.

11. You will need to calculate the amount to be entered into Federal Income Tax Expense using a nested "IF" ⌘ statement. To minimize future changes to the nested "IF" statement, insert a new worksheet and name it "**Reference Data.**" Create a heading in this worksheet for Corporate Tax Brackets and Rates. You should provide any text necessary for the bracket descriptions in column A (e.g., "Greater than or equal to," etc.), the amounts for the brackets in column B (e.g., $50,000, etc.) and the rates in column C (e.g., 15%, etc.). Creating the brackets and associated rates will take some thought on your part as they are to be used in your nested IF statement for the corporate tax

calculation to eliminate the need to recreate the formula if the brackets or rates are changed by Congress at a later date.

12. Create names ⌘ for the brackets and the rates (e.g., Bracket0, Rate0, Bracket1, Rate1, etc.)

13. Create the nested IF ⌘ statement using the cell names on the Reference Data sheet.

14. Create the following range names ⌘ for the Statement of Income and Retained Earnings:
    - Cost_Of_Goods_Sold
    - Net_Sales
    - Interest_Expense
    - NIBT (i.e., net income before tax)
    - Federal_Income_Tax
    - Net_Income

15. Use formulas to calculate subtotals and totals on the income statement.

16. Be sure to include Earnings Per Share on your income statement. There are 45,000 shares issued and outstanding.

17. Insert a new worksheet entitled "**Balance Sheet**" and create a **comparative, classified Balance Sheet** employing the same general formatting techniques and utilizing formulas as before (see *Figure 4*). Determine your column widths as you deem appropriate. Use a single column to present the various account balances for 2002 and 2003.

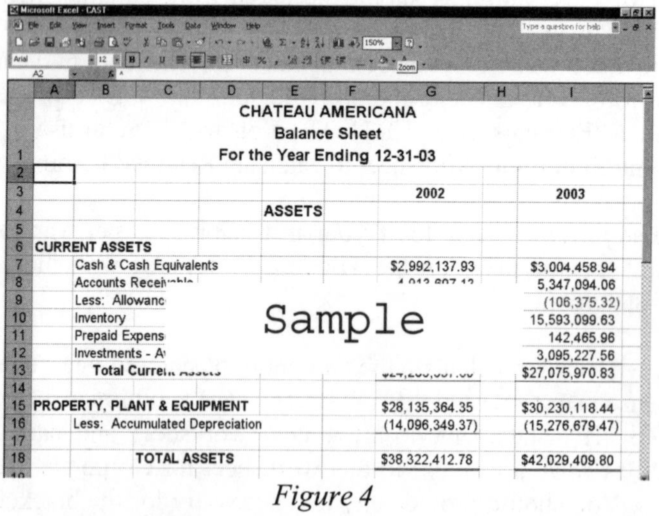

Figure 4

18. Create the following range names for the Balance Sheet:
    - Beginning_Inventory
    - Ending_Inventory
    - Current_Assets (for 2003 only)

- Beginning_Total_Assets
- Ending_Total_Assets
- Current_Liabilities (for 2003 only)
- Beginning_Stockholders_Equity
- Ending_Stockholders_Equity

Data Integrity Tutorial

Adjusting column width. Columns may be formatted using the **Format > Column > Width** menu or by adjusting the width using the cursor. Place the cursor on the line separating the heading for columns A and B on the gray bar above the cells. You will notice that the cursor turns to a cross and the column width is displayed in the box above the column separator. Drag the cursor to the desired width. Repeat for every column whose width should be changed.

Adjusting row height. Rows may be formatted using the **Format > Row > Height** menu or by adjusting the height using the cursor. Place the cursor on the line separating rows 1 and 2. You will notice that the cursor turns to a cross and the row height is displayed in the box above the row separator. Drag the cursor to the desired height. Repeat for every row whose height should be changed.

Heading. To enter a multiple line heading in one cell, type the first line. Hold down the **Alt** key and hit the **Enter** key to go on to the second line, and repeat this process for the third line. To center the heading across columns, highlight the cells in which you would like to center the heading and click on the **Merge and Center** button. Increase the font on each line to the desired size. Resize the height of the row.

Formatting numbers and currency. Click **Format > Cell**. Select **Number** and make sure the **Decimal places** box has "2" and the **Use 1000 Separator (,)** box has a check to format for commas with two decimal points or select **Currency** and make sure the **Decimal places** box has "2" and the **Symbol** box has "$" to format for currency with two decimal points.

Underlining. To underline totals and subtotals use the border Icon. After placing the cursor in the appropriate cell, pull down the border menu by placing the cursor on the arrow next to the Icon and select the dark solid line in the second row, second column.

Another way to place a border in a cell is to select the cell by clicking on it with the right mouse button to bring up the ShortCut Menu, select **Format Cells > Border > Bottom** and choose the heavy dark line under **Style**.

Cell name. When using cell names, you must use underlines ("_") rather than spaces between words. To enter a cell name, first highlight the cell or cells that you wish to name. Use only those cells that contain the numbers you want to name. It is not necessary to include the cells with the text describing those numbers. From the toolbar menu select **Insert > Name > Define** and use the appropriate cell or range name.

Data Integrity Tutorial (continued)

Entering and using formulas. A formula always begins with an "=" sign. Formulas use an operator (+ - / * > < % etc.) combined with values which can be cell references or range names. Note that the following are only examples of formulas you might need:

    =Gross_Revenue-SUM(Sales_Adjustments)
    =C15+C16
    =$E9-$E19
    =SUM(C24:C32)

Note the "**$**" in the third example above. This has the effect of holding the column **E** as an absolute reference; in other words, if this formula is moved to another place in the worksheet, it will still reference column **E** but the row number will change. If a dollar sign is placed on either side of the **E (E9)**, both the column and row reference will be absolute. Without the dollar signs, EXCEL treats cell references as relative; that is, when they are moved, the references will change relative to the new cell position.

To enter a formula in a cell:
  a) Select the cell into which you want to enter the formula.
  b) Type an "=" to activate the formula bar.
  c) Type the formula. If you make a mistake, edit to correct it.
  d) Press Enter or click on the enter box (the green checkmark) next to the formula bar.

Renaming a sheet. Double click on the Sheet tab at the bottom of the screen and enter Income Statement or other appropriate name.

Nested "IF" statement. An "IF" statement returns one of two values based on a specified logical condition. For example, if X is less than Y then return the value of 5 else return the value of 10. "IF" statements begin with the "=" sign and use comparison operators (=, >, <, >=, <=, <>) to specify the logical condition. The format for an "IF" statement is:
      "=IF(**A1**<=**B1**,**C1**,**D1**)."

This "IF" statement specifies that if cell **A1** is less than or equal to cell **B1** (logical condition) then return the value in cell **C1** else return the value in cell **D1**. Note that numerical values, cell references or range names can be used in "IF" statements. A nested "IF" statement returns one of three or more values based on specified logical conditions. For example, if X is greater than Y then return the value of 10 else if X is greater than Z then return the value of 5 else return the value of 1. The format for a nested "IF" statement is:
      "=IF(**A1**>=**B1**,**A2**, IF(**A1**>=**C1**,**B2**,**C2**))."

This "IF" statement specifies that if cell **A1** is greater than or equal to cell **B1** (first logical condition) then return the value in cell **A2** else if cell **A1** is greater than or equal to cell **C1** (second logical condition) then return the value in cell **B2** else return the value in cell **C2**.

DATA ANALYSIS

With the data you now have in the financial statements and with the cell names that you have created in those financial statements, it is very easy to calculate some common ratios.

Requirements

1. Open the **CA_excel** file and insert a new worksheet entitled "**Ratio Analysis**."

2. On this new worksheet, calculate the ratios listed below by using formulas that refer to cell or range names that you have created. Do not use direct cell references (e.g., N42, G18, etc.) in these calculations.

   - Current ratio
   - Inventory turnover
   - Asset turnover
   - Return on equity
   - Debt to equity ratio
   - Times interest earned

   By using cell names only you increase the flexibility of your Excel workbook. For example, rows and columns can more easily be inserted and deleted without altering cell and range names, or formulas that refer to them.

3. Format your Ratio Analysis worksheet such that one column contains the ratio name and one column contains the ratio itself. In addition, the spreadsheet should include an appropriate heading.

INFORMATION NEEDS

Information needs vary among the users of the accounting information system and information overload is a very real problem in businesses. Spreadsheets are very flexible and have very powerful reporting capabilities. Using the spreadsheets and the financial statements you have prepared, you can easily report information to each user according to his or her needs by grouping and ungrouping data from a single spreadsheet without changing the format of the spreadsheet. For example, a company's president may only want to see the overall picture, rather than the detail of the accounts, while the vice president of sales might want to see details related to a specific product or line of products.

Spreadsheets can also be used to sort and query large bodies of data to extract only the desired information. For example, the controller may want to see a listing of only those expense accounts that exceed a certain dollar amount.

The following requirements will help you create an outline for the income statement that will let you show or hide varying levels of detail without changing the income statement format itself.

Requirements

1. Open the **CA_excel** file and click on the **Income Statement** worksheet. Highlight columns B through E.

2. Click on **Data > Group and Outline > Group**. Notice that a bar with a minus sign appears above the column letters.

3. Click on the minus sign to see what happens.

4. Highlight rows 6 through 8 and repeat the **Group** command.

5. Repeat the **Group** command for "OPERATING EXPENSES" and "OTHER INCOME AND EXPENSES" (see *Figure 5*).

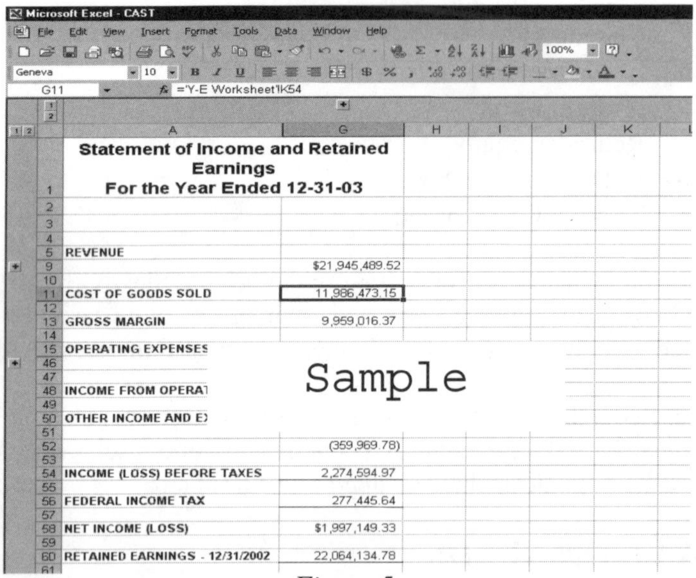

Figure 5

Now assume that the CFO has heard about your Excel skills and has asked you to help him determine which of the expense accounts for Chateau Americana, Inc. exceeded $200,000 for 2003. Filter the expense accounts to provide this information as follows:

6. Insert a new worksheet entitled "**Operating Expenses**" into the **CA_excel** file. For all operating expenses copy the account title and amount from the **Y-E Worksheet** to the new worksheet.

7. Insert a row at the top of the data and enter the column headings "**Operating Expenses**" in cell **A1** and "**Amount**" in cell **B1**.

8. Extract, or filter, all operating expenses in excess of $200,000 ⌘. Create an appropriate heading for the worksheet (see *Figure 6*).

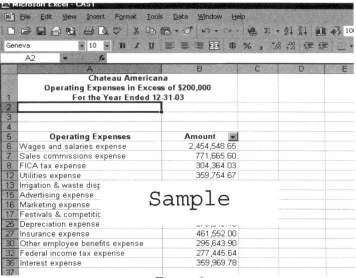

Figure 6

Information Needs Tutorial

Filtering data. Highlight the cells to be filtered including cells containing descriptions for other cells. Go to **Data** > **Filter** > **Auto Filter**. Notice that arrows for the pull-down menus appear in the top cells. Click on the arrow in the column to be filtered to obtain the appropriate pull-down menu. Select **Custom** from the pull-down menu. In the **Custom** window, click on the pull-down menu next to the box containing "equal" to select the appropriate logical condition and input the appropriate amount in the box to the right.

NOTE: You can restore the worksheet to its original format by selecting **Data** > **Filter** and removing the checkmark on **Auto Filter**. Therefore, it is not necessary to copy the data you are filtering to a new worksheet although it is advisable such that you are sure that you do not permanently alter the original format in any way.

DATABASE FUNCTIONS

One of the benefits of a database is the reduction or elimination of data redundancy, which in turn, reduces or eliminates data inconsistency. This is one of the reasons you have been instructed to use formulas whenever possible. **VLOOKUP** is an Excel function that queries data found on one or more worksheets and returns the query results to another worksheet, thus eliminating the need to reenter the data.

Requirements

1. Open the **CA_excel** file and insert a new worksheet. Name the new worksheet "**Payroll Master File.**"

2. On a blank the Payroll Master File, build a payroll rate table (beginning in cell **A1**) with the following headings: **ID, EMPLOYEE NAME, PAY TYPE, PAY RATE**, and **FIT W/H** (i.e., the amount of federal income tax to be withheld).

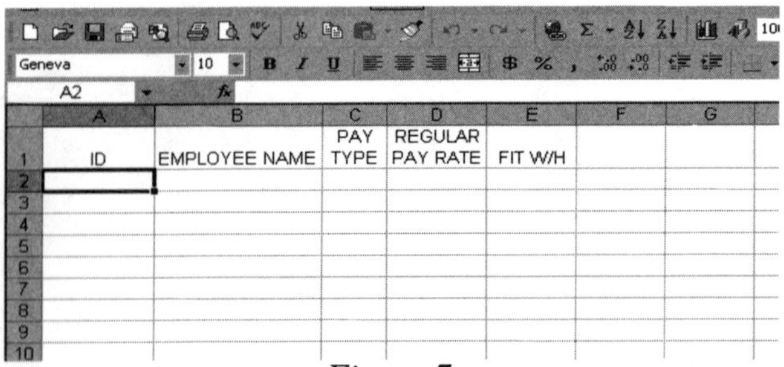

Figure 7

3. Use the following information to enter the data in the **Payroll Master File** worksheet:

Employee Name	Social Security Number	Pay Type	Regular Pay Rate	Filing Status	FIT W/H Allowance
Rodriguez, José G.	124-11-7755	Salaried	2550.00	Married	4
Johnson, Anna C.	296-49-3438	Salaried	1750.00	Married	3
Hissom, Robert T.	349-43-6417	Hourly	14.25	Single	0
Bryan, Thomas P.	014-39-4215	Hourly	15.00	Single	1

NOTE: The employee ID is the employee's social security number. The pay type is "S" for salaried employees or "H" for hourly employees. The FIT withholding should be the amount of federal income tax withheld for the pay period ending December 31, 2003. If you have not already completed the *Manual AIS Module*, you will need to determine the proper amount of federal income tax withheld for each employee by using the Wage Bracket Tables. This information can be found in IRS Publication 15.

4. The **Payroll Master File** worksheet will be used as a database for the **Payroll Journal** worksheet provided for you in the **CA_excel** file. To accomplish this, you must designate an array for the database (i.e., create a range name). To do this, highlight cells **A2:E5** and designate the range name (i.e., array) as **PAYROLL_MASTER.**

5. For each employee in the payroll subsidiary ledgers, enter the payroll pay date (December 31, 2003) and employee ID in cells **A3** through **B6** on the **Payroll Journal** worksheet.

NOTE: The **Payroll Journal** worksheet has already been created and formatted, but does not contain any data, formulas, or functions. However, the worksheet does contain various range names which you must use in creating the required formulas and functions.

6. Use the **VLOOKUP** function ⌘ in cells **C3** and **D3** in the **Payroll Journal** worksheet to return the employee's name and pay type to these cells.

NOTE: The **Payroll Journal** worksheet requires no entry for salaried employees in columns **E** or **H.** However, entries for the regular and overtime hours worked will be required later when entering the data for hourly employees.

7. Use the **VLOOKUP** function to return the pay rate in cell **F3** in the **Payroll Journal** worksheet.

8. In the **Payroll Journal** worksheet, create formulas to calculate the regular pay and overtime pay for cells **G3** and **I3**, respectively. **HINT:** These formulas must contain an **IF** statement based upon the time unit that accommodates salaried employees who do not have entries for number of hours worked.

9. In the **Payroll Journal** worksheet, create formulas in cells **J3** and **K3** to calculate gross pay and FICA, respectively.

10. Use the **VLOOKUP** function in cell **L3** in the **Payroll Journal** worksheet to return the amount of federal income tax to be withheld.

11. In the **Payroll Journal** worksheet, create a formula in cell **M3** to calculate net pay and enter the appropriate check number in cell **N3** beginning with check number **7111**.

12. For internal control purposes, a formula should also be created in cell **N4** in the **Payroll Journal** worksheet as a sequential number check for the check number (i.e., "=N3 +1").

13. To facilitate the entry of payroll data for any other employees, you will need to copy the formulas and functions you created. For this assignment, you only need to copy them into the next 3 rows.

Database Functions Tutorial

VLOOKUP function. The VLOOKUP function in EXCEL searches a previously defined database (i.e., array designated by an appropriate range name) for a specified value and returns a desired field (i.e., a data value) from that database. The syntax for the VLOOKUP function is

=VLOOKUP(lookup_value,table_array,col_index_num,range_lookup)

where

lookup_value names the value to be matched in the database. The **lookup_value** is typically a value that is unique to each row of data. For example, in a customer database, the **lookup_value** might be the Customer ID number. Therefore, in an employee database, the **lookup_value** would be the Employee ID number.

table_array provides the name of the database that stores the data you want to bring into the current worksheet.

> **col_index_num** specifies the column number in the database in which the desired data value is located (NOTE: you must count the columns beginning with A=1, etc., and enter the appropriate column number).
>
> **range_lookup** is a logical value specifying whether or not you want an exact match; FALSE indicates an exact match is desired; TRUE indicates that an approximate match may be returned.

INTRODUCTION TO PIVOTTABLES

You have been asked to prepare Chateau Americana's budget for next year. You should create the budget in a way that takes advantage of Excel's ability to simplify data analysis. You decide to utilize a PivotTable to assist in this effort.

A PivotTable is an interactive table that enables you to quickly sift through and summarize large amounts of data. You can rotate rows and columns to see different summaries of the source data, filter the data by displaying different pages, or display details for certain areas of interest.

Before creating a PivotTable, you must prepare the data source. An excerpt from the Chateau Americana budget has been provided for you. You will find it on the "**Master Budget**" worksheet contained in the CA_excel file. Certain assumptions have been made and constraints have been imposed to facilitate your handling of the budget and the PivotTable, as detailed below.

The budget contains data for the first 6 months and contains only selected accounts. For purposes of this assignment, only three departments have been selected and the number of employees per department has been limited, as follows:

> Administration (Edward and Rob)
> Marketing (Taylor, Daniel and Cameron)
> Operations (Jacques and Paul)

Review the **Master Budget** worksheet. Notice that the worksheet has the following headings: **ACCT_TYPE, ACCT_CODE, ACCT_TITLE, DEPT, COST_CENTER, YR, MON, BUDGET, EXPLANATIONS**. These represent the fields that you will use to create the PivotTable.

Requirements

1. Open the **CA_excel** file and click on the **Master Budget** worksheet. Be sure that the cursor is placed somewhere in the data on the worksheet. From the main menu at the top of the screen, select **Data > PivotTable and PivotChart Report**. The PivotTable Wizard, Step 1 of 3 screen appears (see *Figure 8*). Be sure that the radio buttons for "Microsoft Excel list or database" and for "PivotTable" are selected. Click on **Next**.

2. Step 2 of 3: Be sure that the entire master budget has been selected (the range should be **A1** to **I151**). Click on **Next**.

3. Step 3 of 3: Be sure that the radio button for "New worksheet" is selected. Click on **Finish**.

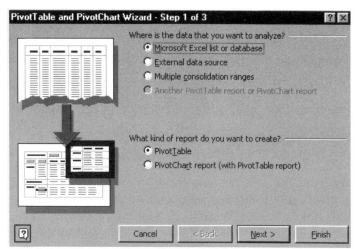

Figure 8

4. Notice that Excel has generated (and moved you to) a new worksheet to create the PivotTable. You should see a **Drop** table and a **PivotTable Field List** that contains the column headings from your **Master Budget** spreadsheet (see *Figure 9*).

   Drag these headings into the box as follows:

   > **ACCT_CODE** into the **Drop Row Fields Here** area.

   > **BUDGET** into the **Drop Data Items Here** area. (**NOTE:** The tab above **ACCT_CODE** should now say "**Sum of BUDGET**" rather than **BUDGET**. A list of general ledger codes should appear with a total beside it. The total at the bottom of the sheet should be $2,266,066. Excel has now generated a PivotTable that summarized the master budget by GL code.

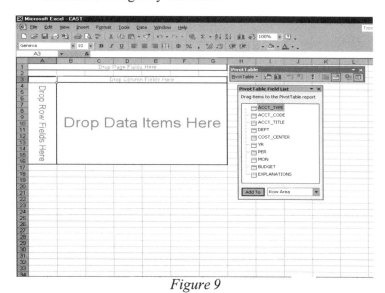

Figure 9

5. Notice that the **Master Budget** worksheet is still intact. Now rename the new worksheet "**Pivot**".

6. General ledger codes do not provide much information without the account titles. To add the general ledger account titles, right click anywhere within the PivotTable that you just created to access the short-cut menu.

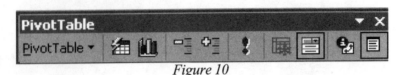

Figure 10

In the **PivotTable** short-cut menu, click on the **PivotTable** pull-down menu. From this menu, select **Wizard**. A window containing Step 3 of 3 of the Wizard should appear. Click on **Layout**. The **Column-Row-Data** box re-appears (see *Figure 11*).

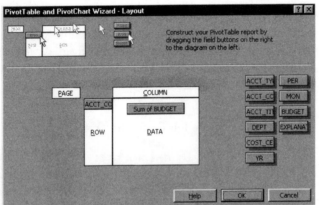

Figure 11

7. Drag and drop **ACCT_TITLE** below **ACCT_CODE** in the **Row** area. Then click **OK** and click on **Finish.**

8. The general ledger codes, descriptions and their totals are now in the PivotTable. This contains much more detail than we need in the budget. For example, the total lines are repetitious and should be removed. To do this, right click on the **ACCT_CODE** field button (this should be in Cell **A4**) to access the short-cut menu. Select **Field Settings** to pull up the **PivotTable Field** window. In the **Subtotals** area on the left, click on the radio button for **None.** This should deselect the **Automatic** button. Click on **OK** and the subtotals disappear.

9. Left justify the GL account codes by highlighting column **A** (left click on the **A** at the top of the column) and clicking the **Align Left** ■ icon.

10. To provide managers with more detailed budget information, the period should be added to the PivotTable. Right click anywhere within the

PivotTable. Select **Wizard**. Click on **Layout**. The **Column-Row-Data** box re-appears. Drop **MON** into the **Column** area. Then click **OK** and click on **Finish**. The PivotTable should now break down the GL account totals by month.

11. Pull up the **Column-Row-Data** box again. Drag and drop **ACCT_TYPE** above **ACCT_CODE** (the **Row** area now contains **ACCT_TYPE**, **ACCT_CODE** and **ACCT_TITLE**). Click **OK** and click on **Finish**. The PivotTable should now be divided into '601 – **Salaries**", '602 – **Payroll Taxes**," "610 – **Occupancy**," etc, each with a total.

12. The PivotTable allows you to easily compare values in the same category or field through the use of structured selection by highlighting each of the total lines. To see how this works, go to cell **B6** and right click in that cell. Click on **Select – Enable Selection** (see *Figure 12*).

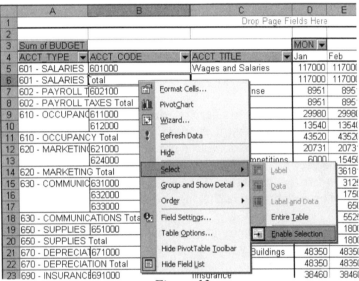

Figure 12

13. Then click on the yellow "**Fill Color**" icon. Now click anywhere on the table. The "**Total**" lines are now shaded yellow (see *Figure 13*).

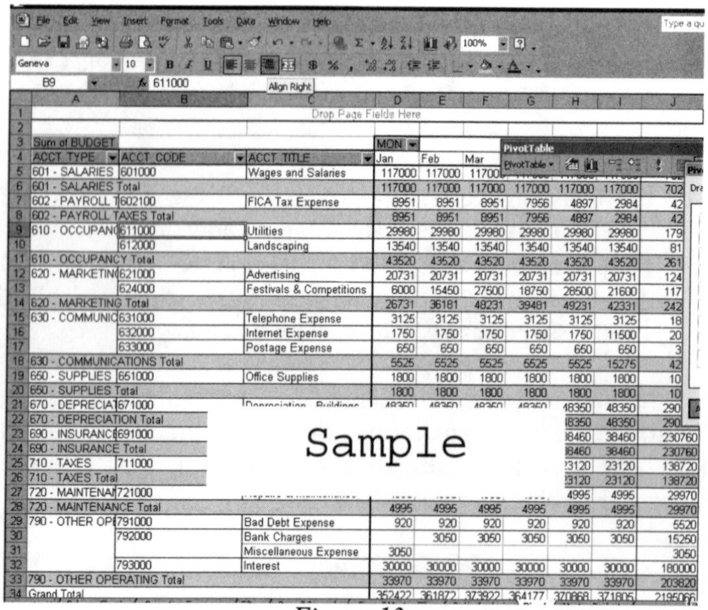

	A	B	C	D	E	F	G	H	I	J
1	Drop Page Fields Here									
2										
3	Sum of BUDGET			MON						
4	ACCT TYPE	ACCT CODE	ACCT TITLE	Jan	Feb	Mar				
5	601 - SALARIES	601000	Wages and Salaries	117000	117000	11700				
6	601 - SALARIES Total			117000	117000	117000	117000	117000	117000	702
7	602 - PAYROLL T	602100	FICA Tax Expense	8951	8951	8951	7956	4897	2984	42
8	602 - PAYROLL TAXES Total			8951	8951	8951	7956	4897	2984	42
9	610 - OCCUPANC	611000	Utilities	29980	29980	29980	29980	29980	29980	179
10		612000	Landscaping	13540	13540	13540	13540	13540	13540	81
11	610 - OCCUPANCY Total			43520	43520	43520	43520	43520	43520	261
12	620 - MARKETIN	621000	Advertising	20731	20731	20731	20731	20731	20731	124
13		624000	Festivals & Competitions	6000	15450	27500	18750	28500	21600	117
14	620 - MARKETING Total			26731	36181	48231	39481	49231	42331	242
15	630 - COMMUNIC	631000	Telephone Expense	3125	3125	3125	3125	3125	3125	18
16		632000	Internet Expense	1750	1750	1750	1750	1750	11500	20
17		633000	Postage Expense	650	650	650	650	650	650	3
18	630 - COMMUNICATIONS Total			5525	5525	5525	5525	5525	15275	42
19	650 - SUPPLIES	651000	Office Supplies	1800	1800	1800	1800	1800	1800	10
20	650 - SUPPLIES Total			1800	1800	1800	1800	1800	1800	10
21	670 - DEPRECIA1	671000	Depreciation - Buildings	48350	48350	48350	48350	48350	48350	290
22	670 - DEPRECIATION Total							48350	48350	290
23	690 - INSURANCE	691000						38460	38460	230760
24	690 - INSURANCE Total							38460	38460	230760
25	710 - TAXES	711000						23120	23120	138720
26	710 - TAXES Total							23120	23120	138720
27	720 - MAINTENAN	721000						4995	4995	29970
28	720 - MAINTENANCE Total			4995	4995	4995	4995	4995	4995	29970
29	790 - OTHER OPE	791000	Bad Debt Expense	920	920	920	920	920	920	5520
30		792000	Bank Charges		3050	3050	3050	3050	3050	15250
31			Miscellaneous Expense	3050						3050
32		793000	Interest	30000	30000	30000	30000	30000	30000	180000
33	790 - OTHER OPERATING Total			33970	33970	33970	33970	33970	33970	203820
34	Grand Total			352422	361872	373922	364177	370868	371805	2195066

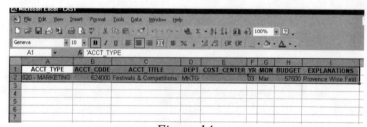

Figure 13

DETAIL IN REPORTING

The PivotTable allows the user to query or "drilldown" into a particular value in the PivotTable report to examine that item more closely. This provides a great deal of power and flexibility to the PivotTable report, whether the report is for budgeting applications, reporting monthly costs to department managers, or for reporting the results of sales to territory managers. The user can query a balance to view any of the underlying detail by simply double clicking on the entry in question.

The CFO has asked you to identify any unusual items in the budgeted amounts and report them to him. A quick review of the budget reveals two months under **Festivals and Competitions** and one month under **Internet and Computer** that appear to have unusual amounts of expenditures.

Requirements

1. Open the **CA_excel** file and click on the **Pivot** worksheet. To determine what has caused this spike in costs, query one of the amounts in question by double clicking on grand total amount. A new worksheet appears that provides detail for the amount in question (see *Figure 14*).

	A	B	C	D	E	F	G	H	I
1	ACCT TYPE	ACCT CODE	ACCT TITLE	DEPT	COST CENTER	YR	MON	BUDGET	EXPLANATIONS
2	620 - MARKETING	624000	Festivals & Competitions	MKTG		03	Mar	57500	Provence Wine Fest

Figure 14

2. Return to the **Pivot** worksheet. Examine the amounts in the other questioned account. Double click on the grand total amount to investigate the cause.

   Return to the **Pivot** worksheet again. You may also want to limit other users' abilities to drilldown into the data. This is done by right-clicking anywhere in the PivotTable report, selecting **Table Options** from the shortcut menu, and deselecting the **Enable drill to details** box.

3. As you've seen, the PivotTable can be used to display only the data of interest. You might, for example, want to view the data for a particular department rather than for all departments or view data by cost centers. Either of these views can be obtained by dropping a particular field of interest in the **Column** area of the PivotTable or by filtering the entire PivotTable report to display data for a single item or all the items, using the **Page** field.

   Access the **Column-Row-Data** box again. Remove **MON** from **Column** by dropping it anywhere outside the box. Drag and drop **DEPT** into the **Column** area. Click **OK** and click on **Finish**. Notice that the departmental totals for the Administrative, Marketing, and Operations departments now appear.

4. You can also view the data by department and month by using the **"Page"** fields. Open the **COLUMN-ROW-DATA** box again. Drag **DEPT** to the **Page** area and drop it. Drag and drop **MON** back into the **Column** area. Click **OK** and click on **Finish**. Notice that the data is now broken down by period again. Notice also that cell **A1** now contains a grey box entitled **"DEPT"** and cell **B1** says, **"All"** and has a pull-down menu. **DEPT** is now a **Page** field. It allows the user to see the information for the entire organization or by department (see *Figure 15*).

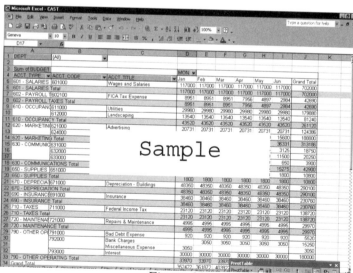

Figure 15

5. Click on the down arrow in the right of cell **B1** and notice that the choices **ADMIN**, **MKTG**, and **OPS** appear. Click on **ADMIN**. The PivotTable now

shows the costs for the Administrative department. You can click on the pull-down arrow again to look at the budgets for the Marketing department and for Operations. Note that the (**All**) option allows you to view the company totals.

6. View the **ADMIN** data again. This data can broken down further into individual cost centers. To do this, access the **Column-Row-Data** box again. Drag and drop **COST_CENTER** below **ACCT_TITLE** and remove the subtotals. The PivotTable is now broken down further to show the costs attributed to the individual cost centers in the Administrative department (i.e., Rob and Edward). Some of the cells in the **COST_CENTER** column contain '**(blank)**." This indicates that the costs for these accounts were not allocated to individual cost centers within the Administrative department, but were allocated instead to the entire Administrative department.

7. As more data is included in a worksheet, the threat of *information overload* or *analysis paralysis* increases. In addition, as more data is included, the PivotTable will likely require more levels to facilitate analysis of the data. However, increasing levels also increases complexity making data analysis more difficult. To address the issue of complexity, the PivotTable can be expanded or collapsed between different levels of detail using the **Hide Detail** and **Show Detail** commands. Click on cell **B1** and select (**All**). The entire budget is now displayed. Right click on **A4**, **ACCT_TYPE**. Select **Group and Show Detail - Hide Detail** from the short-cut menu. Only the top level data (i.e., the account types) should now be visible (see *Figure 16*).

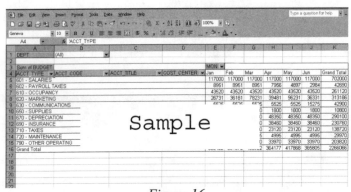

Figure 16

8. The detail can then be expanded for one or more account types. However, before you can access the detail you will need to re-enable the drilldown option that you previously deselected in step 3 above. Show the detail for the costs associated with Communications by double clicking on the "630 – Communications" title in column **A**. The Communications detail is now shown down to the **COST_CENTER** level (see *Figure 17*).

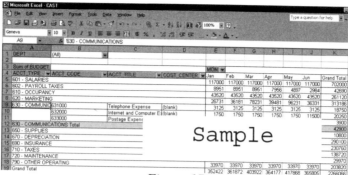

Figure 17

9. To return to the more concise view, double click in the space below the "630 – Communications" title.

10. Return the entire PivotTable to its full detail again by right clicking **ACCT_TYPE**. From the short-cut menu, select **Group and Show Detail - Show Detail**.

11. It is also sometimes desirable to focus on certain periods in a budget. The PivotTable enables you to hide the detail for some periods while leaving the detail for others showing and simultaneously recalculate the cumulative totals to show totals for just the periods of interest. Look at the data for the second quarter only by left clicking on the **MON** title. Uncheck January, February and March and click **OK**. The PivotTable now contains the data only for April, May and June and the cumulative totals for each **ACCT_CODE** have been recalculated to include only the amounts from the second quarter months (see *Figure 18*).

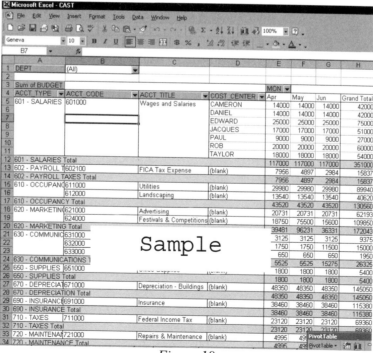

Figure 18

12. Unhide the first quarter months by left clicking on **MON** and reselecting January, February and March and click on **OK**.

FLEXIBLE BUDGETING USING PIVOTTABLES

Flexible budgets are an important tool in accounting. PivotTables facilitate flexible budgeting. It is very easy to make changes, the results appear immediately, and any formulas that are affected are automatically updated. To see how revisions work, perform the following independent steps.

1. Open the **CA_excel** file and click on the **Pivot** worksheet.

2. After the budget was established, it was decided that Daniel would transfer from Marketing to Administration as of March 1. At that time, his salary will increase by $1,000. To adjust the budget for this change, click onto the **Master Budget** worksheet. Since the **ACCT_CODE** filter is still on, click the pull-down menu in that column and select **(All)** to show all the records. Now click on the **Cost Center** pull-down menu and select Daniel. Six records for Daniel should appear. Change Daniel's department for the appropriate periods and increase his salary for those periods (see *Figure 19*).

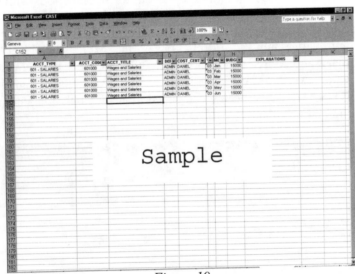

Figure 19

3. Go to the **Pivot** worksheet. Notice that Daniel's salary has not changed. Right click anywhere on the worksheet and click on **Refresh Data** (see *Figure 20*).

4. Go back to the **Master Budget** worksheet. Turn off the **Autofilter** by selecting **Data - Filter - Autofilter** from the menu and clicking on **Autofilter** to deselect it. Insert a new column before the **EXPLANATIONS** column. Copy the **BUDGET** values into the new column **I** by selecting the entire **BUDGET** column and copying and pasting it to the new column. Change the column heading **BUDGET** to **REV_BUDGET**. You should now have the original and revised budgets side by side.

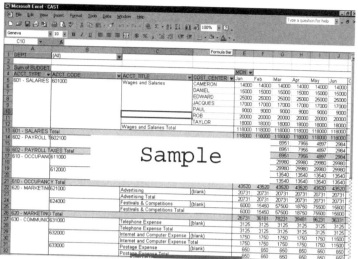

Figure 20

5. Turn on the **Autofilter** again. Select Cameron and update her salary to reflect a $1,000 raise in the **REV_BUDGET** column for June. Click onto the **Pivot** worksheet. Right click on the PivotTable, and select **Refresh Data** from the short-cut menu.

6. Note what happens. Nothing happens because the PivotTable was set up to display the sum of **BUDGET**. Now access the **Column-Row-Data** box and drag and drop **REV_BUDGET** below **BUDGET** in the **Data** area. Click on **OK** and then click on **Finish**. The PivotTable should now display both the original and the revised budget. After comparing the revised budget numbers to the original budget numbers access the **Column-Row-Data** window and remove the **BUDGET** numbers from **Data**.

7. Once the first budget has been created using PivotTables, it can be used to produce others very quickly. In the **PivotTable** worksheet, show all departments. In the **PivotTable** short-cut menu, click on the **PivotTable** pull-down menu. From this menu, select **Show Pages** and click **OK**. The three departmental budget PivotTables (one for **ADMIN**, one for **MKTG** and one for **OPS**) were created as three new worksheets in your workbook. Open the **ADMIN** worksheet. You will notice that columns **A** and **C** need to be widened in this and the other two new worksheets. Adjust these two columns to the appropriate width.

You can widen the columns for all of these new worksheets at one time. To do this, depress the **Shift** key and highlight the departmental sheets by clicking on the **Pivot** worksheet *OR* hold down the **CTRL** key and select each of the departmental sheets individually. Widen columns **A** and **C** by highlighting the columns and selecting **Format - Column - AutoFit Selection**.

8. You have now completed the Excel assignment. Save your work. Your instructor will provide you with the appropriate file naming convention.

EXCEL GENERAL TUTORIAL

The following information provides the novice Excel user with some basic terminology utilized by Excel. If you have not used Excel previously, you should take the time to read through this information.

Excel Workbook

Each Excel file is called a "workbook". Each workbook contains several worksheets. Each of these sheets can be accessed (i.e., you can switch back and forth between them) by clicking on the tabs at the bottom of the Excel window (e.g., switch from "Sheet 1" to "Sheet 2"). Each of these sheets can also be renamed by double-clicking on the appropriate sheet tab.

Help

In addition to the information provided in this assignment, Excel has an excellent Help facility which allows you to learn more about a variety of topics, to see demonstrations on the topic, and to facilitate a transition to Excel for Lotus users. The Help facility also allows you to keep the information on top of the worksheet as you attempt to apply its information to your application (click on the "**On Top**" button in the Help window). Help may be accessed by using the **Menu Bar** or by clicking on the **Help** icon.

Menu Bar

The menu bar contains pull-down menus for all Excel commands. Examine the commands which are located in the pull-down menus under the following broad categories:

> File
> Edit
> View
> Insert
> Format
> Tools
> Data
> Window
> Help

Moving Around a Worksheet

You can move around a worksheet by selecting a cell using the cursor (i.e., pointing at a new cell) or using the arrow keys until you have arrived at the desired cell. You can also use the **Menu Bar** (i.e., **Edit - Go To**) and type in the desired cell address.

Entering Data

Data is entered in a cell by selecting the cell itself, typing the desired data, and (1) hitting the "**Enter**" key or (2) clicking on the enter box (a green "✓" located on the edit bar). You may change your mind about the data you have entered by hitting the "**Escape**" key prior to (1) or (2) above.

Editing Data

Previously entered data may be edited by accessing the edit bar. This may be done by selecting the desired cell, hitting the **"F2"** key, using the arrow keys or the cursor to arrive at the point in the cell which needs to be edited and making the changes, and hitting the **"Enter"** key or the enter box. Alternatively, editing may be done by double-clicking on the desired cell to bring up the edit line, using the cursor to arrive at the point of insertion, and proceeding as above. You may exit the edit mode without making any changes by hitting the "**Escape**" key.

Moving Data

Data can be moved by copying it from one cell to another or by cutting it out of one cell and pasting it in a new cell.

> **Copying data** - Data can be copied by selecting the desired cell or cells and (1) using the **Menu Bar** (i.e., **Edit - Copy**); (2) clicking on the right mouse button to bring down the shortcut menu and selecting "**Copy**"; or (3) if you are copying the data to an adjacent cell, you can use the "**Fill Handle**" and drag the cursor to the adjacent cell.

> **Moving data** - Data can be moved by selecting the desired cell or cells and (1) using the **Menu Bar** (i.e., **Edit - Cut**), moving to the new desired cell and accessing the **Menu Bar** again (i.e., **Edit - Paste**); (2) clicking on the right mouse button to bring down the shortcut menu and selecting "**Cut**" and then repeating the process at the new desired cell and selecting "**Paste**"; and (3) positioning the pointer over the border of the selected cell or cells and dragging the border to the new location.

Selecting Multiple Cells

You may wish to have your commands apply to more than one cell. Multiple cells may be selected in several ways.

> **Highlighting a range of cells** - Position your cursor in the cell in the upper left hand corner of the range of cells you wish to manipulate and drag it down to the lower right hand corner of the range. Then apply whatever command you wish for that range of cells.

> **Highlighting a column or a row** - You may apply your command to an entire column or row by positioning the cursor on the column or row header and clicking on the letter or number (you will notice that the entire column/row is then highlighted).

Arithmetic Operations on Data Cells

You may add, subtract, multiply, or divide the data in two or more cells by selecting an empty cell and typing an "=" sign, clicking on the first cell you want to be included in the arithmetic formula, selecting the operation's sign (i.e., +, -, *, /), clicking on the second cell to be included, followed by another operation sign if applicable, etc.

You may also use the SUM function to add a group of cells together and use that total in an arithmetic operation (e.g., =SUM(A1:A5)/A7).

NOTE: Excel utilizes the normal order of arithmetic procedures; i.e., multiplication and division operations take precedence over addition and subtraction operations. For example, let's look at possible answers for combinations of operations for the following information:

A1 = 5
A2 = 3
A3 = 15
A4 = 17
A5 = 20
A7 = 4

If your formula reads:	Excel's answer is:
= A1+A2+A3+A4+A5/A7	45
= (A1+A2+A3+A4+A5)/A7	15
=SUM(A1:A5)/A7	15

Other Helpful Information

Row/Column Insertion and deletion - To insert or delete an entire row or column, click on that row's/column's header (i.e., row number/column letter) using the right mouse button and select **Insert** or **Delete**.

Erasing the contents of a cell - Click on the desired cell(s) and hit the **Delete** key.

GENERAL LEDGER APPLICATIONS USING *PEACHTREE COMPLETE ACCOUNTING 2004* ®:
The Winery At Chateau Americana

LEARNING OBJECTIVES

After completing and discussing this assignment, you should be able to:

- Recognize the managerial and technological issues associated with the implementation of a general ledger package
- Complete sample transactions
- Understand the implications of the design of the user interface
- Recognize and evaluate the strengths and weaknesses of controls embedded in a general ledger package
- Compare and contrast a general ledger package with a manual accounting information system

BACKGROUND

As the winery has grown, Rob Breeden, the chief financial officer, has realized that management does not have timely information about the financial condition of the company. This has resulted in several instances in which the decisions made were not optimal. Therefore, he has determined that it is time to convert the current system to a general ledger package. After investigating the possibilities, he has decided to utilize *Peachtree Complete Accounting 2004®*. Chateau Americana has hired you to convert the system.

REQUIREMENTS

Using the *Peachtree Complete Accounting 2004®* software program contained in your *CAST* package or in your school computer lab, you are to convert Chateau Americana from a manual system to a general ledger software package. If you are working on this assignment on your home computer, load the software following the instructions contained on the CD envelope.

As with any other computer file, it is important to **back up frequently** to another storage medium.

SETTING UP A NEW COMPANY

Requirements

1. Start *Peachtree Complete Accounting 2004®* and click on **Set up a new company**.

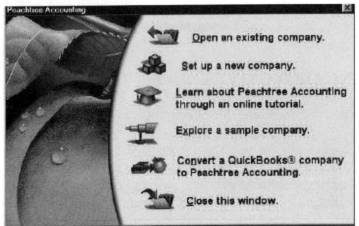

Figure 1

2. The Welcome screen that appears next alerts the user to information that will be required throughout the set-up procedure. Click on **Next**.

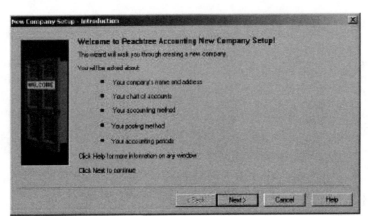

Figure 2

3. Enter the following company information and then click on **Next**:

> The Winery at Chateau Americana, Inc.
> 3003 Vineyard Way
> Huntington, CA 95394
> Phone: (707) 368-8485
> Fax: (707) 368-8486

Do not enter any information in the remaining input boxes.

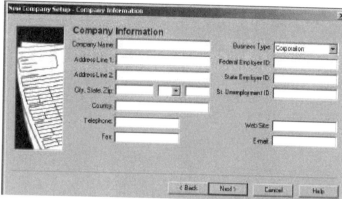

Figure 3

4. You are now asked to select an option for setting up the Chart of Accounts. Peachtree provides you with sample charts of accounts in the event that you are setting up a start-up company. Because Chateau Americana already has a Chart of Accounts select **Build your own company** and click on **Next**.

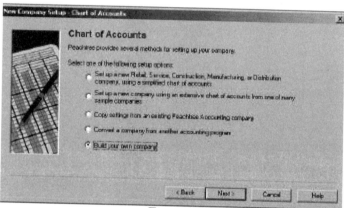

Figure 4

5. The next screen provides options for the company's accounting method. If you examine the Chart of Accounts you will notice various accounts that provide evidence that Chateau Americana utilizes the accrual method of accounting. Therefore, just click on **Next**.

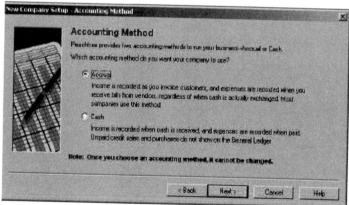

Figure 5

6. Peachtree offers two posting methods. In Real Time mode, each transaction is posted as it is written and the General Ledger is always up to date. In Batch mode, transactions are posted in batches or groups, resulting in processing efficiencies but delaying the updating of the General Ledger. Since one of Rob Breeden's concerns is that of timely information, select the **Real Time** posting method and click on **Next**.

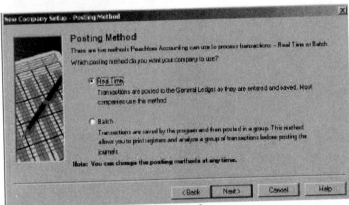

Figure 6

7. The next two screens address the company's accounting period. The first asks you to select the number of accounting periods within a year. The company's fiscal year is a calendar year with 12-monthly accounting periods. Make sure the correct accounting period is selected and click on **Next**.

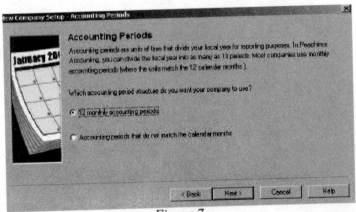

Figure 7

8. Now you are prompted to provide the month and year that the fiscal year begins (i.e., January 2003) and for the first month in which data will be entered. You have been given the general ledger balances as of December 15, 2003. Therefore, the first data will be entered as of December 2003 and payroll will begin as of 2003. Make sure the correct information is input and click on **Next**.

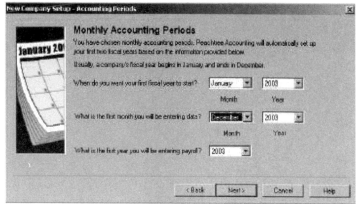

Figure 8

9. You have now completed the set-up procedures for converting Chateau Americana to Peachtree. Click on **Finish**.

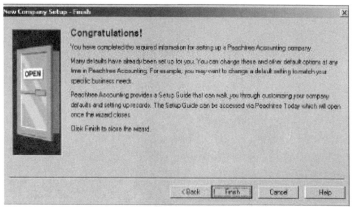

Figure 9

10. The **Peachtree Today** window appears with an arrow pointing to the **Setup Guide**. Click on the **Setup Guide** to proceed.

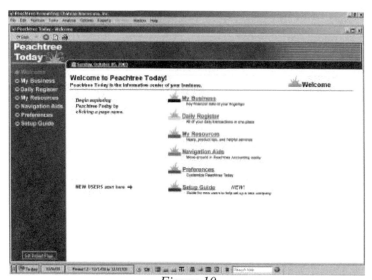

Figure 10

11. If you wish, you may close the file at this time and Peachtree will automatically save the contents.

SETTING UP THE GENERAL LEDGER

Requirements

1. Open the Chateau Americana file. (Note: Peachtree will automatically save the file you created in the first portion of this assignment with the company name you provide. For simplicity, we refer to the company, and file, as Chateau Americana.) Once you click on the **Setup Guide**, you will have access to the General Ledger, Accounts Receivable, Accounts Payable, Payroll, Inventory, and Jobs.

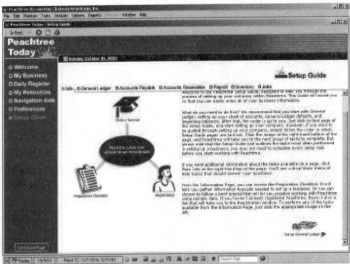

Figure 11

2. You will begin by setting up the **General Ledger.** Click on the **General Ledger** menu selection at the top of the page.

3. You can now set up your **Chart of Accounts**. It is extremely important that you set up the chart of accounts properly. Use the account numbers and related descriptions that follow. (Note: All of the accounts have normal balances)

Account Title	Account #	12/15/03 Balance
Assets (100000)		
General Checking Account	111000	$ 2,222,927.47
Payroll Checking Account	112000	1,000.00
Money Market Account	113000	782,546.49
Savings Account	114000	51,745.56
Petty Cash	119000	500.00
Accounts Receivable	121000	5,366,670.86
Allowance for Bad Debts	129000	95,401.58

Inventory – Production	141000	$ 11,564,851.56
Inventory – Finished Goods	145000	4,044,046.31
Prepaid Expenses	150000	142,465.96
Land and Buildings	160000	16,358,487.34
Equipment	170000	13,844,881.10
Accumulated Depreciation	180000	15,233,662.97
Investments	191000	3,070,227.56
Liabilities (200000)		
Accounts Payable	210000	4,987,975.79
Federal Income Tax Withheld	222100	66,739.08
FICA Withheld	222200	12,237.64
Medicare Withheld	222300	2,862.01
FICA Payable – Employer	223100	12,237.64
Medicare Payable – Employer	223200	2,862.01
Unemployment Taxes Payable	223300	943.57
Other Accrued Expenses	230000	599,348.98
Federal Income Taxes Payable	235000	0.00
Property Taxes Payable	236000	0.00
Mortgages Payable	240000	7,639,067.73
Notes Payable	261000	841,000.00
Owners' Equity (300000)		
Common Stock	310000	90,000.00
Paid-in Capital in Excess of Par – Common	311000	3,567,265.00
Dividends – Common	312000	0.00
Retained Earnings	390000	22,064,134.78
Income (400000)		
Sales	410000	22,264,431.15
Sales Discounts	420000	346,741.36
Sales Returns and Allowances	430000	15,588.47
Gain/Loss – Marketable Securities	452000	0.00
Dividend Income	491000	4,000.00
Interest Income	492000	23,482.56
Cost of Goods Sold	510000	11,514,092.11
Expenses (600000 – 700000)		
Wages and Salaries Expense	601000	1,965,164.11
Sales Commission Expense	601500	771,665.60
FICA Tax Expense	602100	244,124.52
Medicare Tax Expense	602200	57,093.62
FUTA Expense	602300	7,392.00
SUTA Expense	602400	22,176.00
Utilities Expense	611000	307,067.05
Irrigation & Waste Disposal Expense	611300	230,910.91
Landscaping Expense	612000	142,475.69
Advertising Expense	621000	296,794.33
Marketing Expense	623000	192,865.67
Festivals & Competitions Expense	624000	238,654.75
Telephone Expense	631000	37,584.73
Internet & Computer Expense	632000	14,475.00
Postage Expense	633000	35,117.66
Legal & Accounting Fees	641000	88,425.50
Other Consulting Fees	643000	12,500.00

Office Supplies Expense	651000	$ 58,689.68
Data Processing Expense	660000	9,743.89
Depreciation Expense	670000	1,092,832.66
Travel and Entertainment Expense	680000	169,405.86
Other Insurance	691000	115,058.55
Medical Insurance	692000	192,154.80
Workmen's Compensation Insurance	693000	139,750.00
Other Employee Benefits Expense	699000	175,643.90
Dues and Subscriptions Expense	700000	32,076.00
Federal Income Tax Expense	711000	857,595.76
Property Tax Expense	712000	19,875.00
Repairs and Maintenance Expense	721000	71,974.93
Automobile Expense	731000	81,493.45
Lease Expense	740000	113,607.56
Bad Debt Expense	791000	0.00
Miscellaneous Expense	792000	26,575.63
Interest Expense	793000	359,915.53

Begin by entering the Cash account. Type the account number (111000) in the field entitled **Account ID** field. Then enter "General Checking Account" in the **Description** field. The pull-down menu next to the **Account Type** field requires you to select the type of account for each account number. **Do not enter balance information** for the accounts at this time.

Click the **Save** button after you enter each account's information. As you enter the account titles, notice that the full title does not always fit in the space provided and you will, therefore, need to abbreviate the descriptions slightly. In addition, the **Account Type** for many of these accounts is obvious. For those which are not obvious, you will need to refer to the information provided below.

- Common Stock and Paid-In Capital in Excess of Par are "Equity-doesn't close" accounts
- Dividends is an "Equity-gets closed" account type
- "Income" accounts include Sales, Sales Returns and Allowances, Sales Discounts Taken, Gain/Loss on Sale of Assets, Gain/Loss on Sale of Securities, Interest/Dividend Income, and Miscellaneous Revenue

You can go back and view or edit your work at any time by clicking on the **View** button and selecting the account that you want to edit.

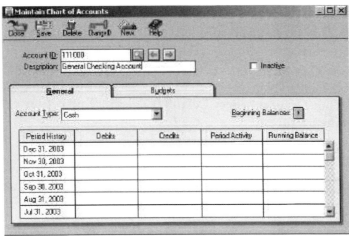

Figure 12

4. When you have finished entering all of the accounts, click the **Close** button. A window will appear asking if you would like to mark the **Setup Guide** as complete. Click **Yes**.

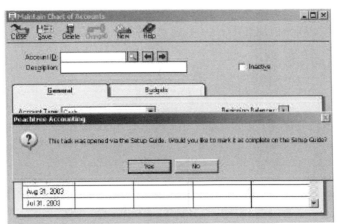

Figure 13

5. If you wish, you may close the file at this time.

SETTING UP BEGINNING ACCOUNT BALANCES

Requirements

1. Open the Chateau Americana file. Click on **Setup Guide** and select the **General Ledger**. Skip Steps 2 and 3 (i.e., **Set Up Your Bank Accounts** and **Select Your General Ledger Defaults**). Click on **Enter Your G/L Account Beginning Balances**.

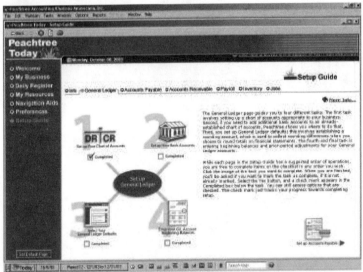

Figure 14

2. Use the balances as of **December 15** provided in the prior section to enter the beginning balances. Select **"From 12/1/2003 through 12/31/2003"** as the period in which to enter beginning balances.

   IMPORTANT: When entering beginning balances, Peachtree classifies the balances as either "Assets, Expenses" accounts that have debit balances or "Liabilities, Equities, Income" accounts that have credit balances. Thus, it is imperative that you watch for contra accounts (e.g., allowance for doubt accounts) and enter them as negative numbers if necessary, since, in most instances, Peachtree will not recognize them as contra accounts.

3. When you are finished entering the beginning balances for all accounts, you should see that the trial balance equals "**0.**" If the trial balance does not equal "**0,**" Peachtree will provide a prompt such as that shown in Figure 15 below.

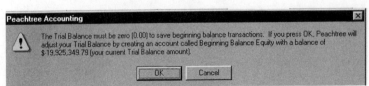

Figure 15

Peachtree will create a temporary equity account for any unaccounted for difference. This amount will have to be investigated and adjusted for at a later time.

4. Click the **OK** button after you have entered all of the account balances and mark the task as completed.

5. If you wish, you may close the file at this time.

SETTING UP ACCOUNTS PAYABLE

Requirements

1. Open the Chateau Americana file. Click on **Setup Guide** and select **Accounts Payable**. You will notice that **Select Your Vendor Defaults** has already been checked off as completed. This is because Peachtree has default settings that you may or may not want to accept for your company. Click on **Select Your Vendor Defaults** to see these defaults. Since the terms vary for each vendor, leave the default set to "Due in number of days." Using the pull-down menu, select the Inventory - Production account for the default Purchases account. The default Discount GL account should also be set to the Inventory - Production account. This sets up the debit for purchases to default to Production Inventory and will similarly credit any discounts to Production Inventory. Clear all remaining default values on the **Payment Terms** tab.

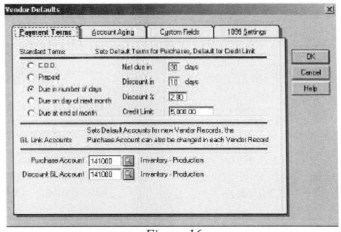

Figure 16

2. Continuing with the vendor defaults menu, click on **Account Aging**. Notice that the default in Peachtree is to age by due date. Change the aging to invoice date and click **OK**. Make certain the task is marked as completed. It will not be necessary to modify any of the fields on the remaining tabs.

3. Click on **Set Up Your Vendors**. Set up the following three vendor accounts using the information provided below along with the vendor invoices provided at the end of this module:

Vendor Name	Vendor ID	Address/Phone
Delicio Vineyards	P2538	12701 South Fernwood Livermore, CA 94550 (925)555-1890
Mendocino Vineyards	P0652	8654 Witherspoon Way Hopland, CA 95449 (707)555-1890
Pacific Gas and Electric	P8325	P.O. Box 2575 San Francisco, CA 94103 (415)973-8943

The **General** data is self-explanatory. If information is not provided above or on the vendor invoices leave the cell blank. Click on the **Purchase Defaults** tab. Make certain that the Production Inventory is shown as the "Purchase Account" for Delicio Vineyards and Mendocino Vineyards. Utilities Expense should be selected as the "Purchase Account" for Pacific Gas and Electric. Select "Best Way" for type of shipping for all vendors. Click **Close** and mark the task as completed. Do not enter any balance information.

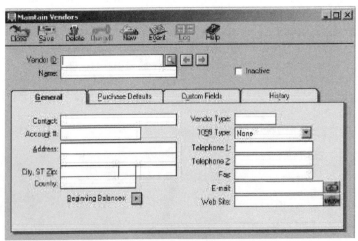

Figure 17

4. Now click on the **Enter Your Vendor Beginning Balances** and enter the beginning balance information for Delicio Vineyards as of December 15. The other two vendors have zero beginning balances. Delicio Vineyards beginning balance information is:

Vendor Name	Invoice Number	Invoice Date	P.O. Number	Amount
Delicio Vineyards	45354	11/04/03	9607	$14,563.56

When you are finished, click **Close** and mark the task as completed.

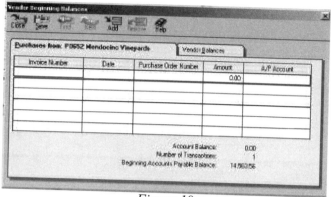

Figure 18

5. If you wish, you may close the file at this time.

SETTING UP ACCOUNTS RECEIVABLE

Requirements

1. Open the Chateau Americana file. Click on **Setup Guide** and select **Accounts Receivable**. **Next,** click on **Select Your Customer Defaults**. Leave the Standard Terms as "Due in number of days." Remove the Credit Limit since you have not been provided credit limits for any of Chateau Americana's customers. Change the Discount Terms to "0" percent and "0" number of days. Set the defaults for the Sales account and the Sales Discounts account using the pull-down menu as you did for Accounts Payable.

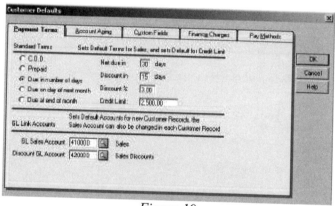

Figure 19

2. Click on the **Account Aging** tab. Change the aging to Invoice date and click **OK**. Mark the task as completed. There is no need to modify any information on the remaining tabs.

3. You do not need to enter anything under **Select Your Statement** and **Invoice Defaults**.

4. Click on **Set Up Your Customers**. Most of the general information required for each of the customers is self-explanatory and can be found below. You may have to refer to purchase orders for any missing information. Chateau Americana makes only wholesale sales to distributors. Therefore, no sales tax is applied to any sales transactions. Do not enter any balance information at this time. Be sure to save each customer as they are entered. After all customers have been entered, dick **Close** and mark the task as completed. There is no need to modify any information on the remaining tabs.

Customer Name	Customer ID	Address/Phone	Terms
Bock Wines and Vines	0501	Pier 19, The Embarcadero San Francisco, CA 94111 Phone: (415) 834-9675	3/15, net 30
California Premium Beverage	0504	39848 South Street Santa Rosa, CA 95402 Phone: (707) 555-7451 Fax: (707) 555-7452	3/15, net 30
Pacific Distribution Co.	0505	10034 Westborough Boulevard San Francisco, CA 94080 Phone: (415) 555-1532	3/15, net 30
Seaside Distributors, Inc.	0506	9835 West Hills Road Ukiah, CA 94080 Phone: (707) 555-3102	3/15, net 30

5. Return to the **Setup Guide** and click on **Enter Your Customer Beginning Balances** and enter the beginning balances (as of December 15). The only customer that has a beginning balance is Pacific Distribution Co. Enter the following beginning balance information for Pacific:

Customer Name	Invoice #	Invoice Date	P.O. #	Amount
Pacific Distribution Co.	15243	11/13/03	123033	$19,576.80

Click on **Close** and mark the task as completed.

6. If you wish, you may close the file at this time.

SETTING UP PAYROLL

Requirements
1. Open the Chateau Americana file. Click on **Setup Guide** and select **Payroll**. Set up the initial payroll fields by clicking on **Select Your Employee Defaults**. The Payroll Setup Wizard window pops up. Go ahead and click **Next**.

Figure 20

2. The following screen informs you of the Tax Table version currently installed on your computer. Click on **Next**. Employees will be paid in California. Assume the unemployment tax rate is 3.2%. Do not record meals and tips. Click on **Next**.

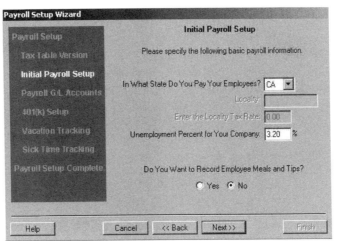

Figure 21

3. You are now prompted to enter the Gross Pay, Tax Liability, and Tax Expense accounts. Select the Wages and Salaries Expense account for the default Gross Pay account. Notice that only one default account can be chosen for the Tax Liability account, despite the fact that companies typically separate the payroll tax liabilities. You will, therefore, have to adjust the default accounts for the payroll tax liabilities later. Select the Federal Income Tax Withheld account for the Tax Liability account and the FICA Tax Expense account for the Tax Expense account. Click on **Next**.

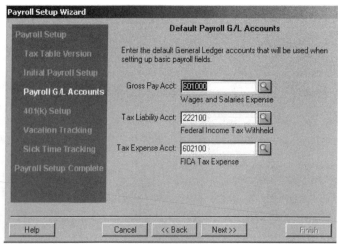

Figure 22

4. You will not set up 401(k) information nor track vacation or sick time so click on **Next** for each of those three windows and then click **Finish**. Notice that the **Employee Defaults** window pops up.

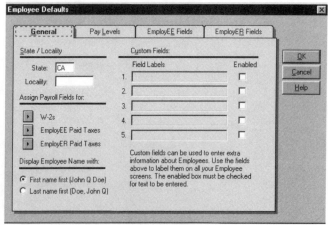

Figure 23

5. Enter the employee default information (**EmployEE Fields**). You will have to select the proper GL accounts for the employee's portion of FICA and Medicare or the amounts will not be properly posted to the correct payable accounts. Be sure to reference Chateau Americana's general ledger to ensure that you understand which payroll accounts are the expense accounts and which are the payable accounts. Remove the check marks from all fields not being used, but do not delete any fields. (**Hint: Remember that Chateau Americana employees only have FIT, FICA, and Medicare withheld from their gross pay**).

6. Enter the employer default information (**EmployER Fields**). Again, be sure that the proper payroll tax payable and expense accounts are being referenced. Remove the check mark from SETT_ER as the state unemployment taxes will be included in SUI_ER. When you are finished, click **OK** and mark the task as completed.

7. Click on **Set up Your Employees** to enter the individual employee's payroll information. Enter the employee's social security number without hyphens as the "Employee ID." Additional information for each employee can be found below:

Name: Thomas P. Bryan			
Social Security No:	014-39-4215	Pay rate:	$15.00
Address:	35 Winchester Street, Huntington, CA 95394	Pay type:	Hourly
Phone:	(707) 555-1495	Position:	Presses
Date of Birth:	6/14/65	Filing Status:	Single
Date of Employment:	4/25/95	Withholding Allowances	1
Date of Last Raise:	4/25/95		

Name: Robert T. Hissom			
Social Security No:	349-43-6417	Pay rate:	$14.25
Address:	3187 Heckert Way, Apt. 4A, Huntington, CA 95394	Pay type:	Hourly
Phone:	(707) 555-1219	Position:	Receiving
Date of Birth:	11/9/77	Filing Status:	Single
Date of Employment:	1/4/98	Withholding Allowances	0
Date of Last Raise:	1/4/03		

Name: Anna C. Johnson			
Social Security No:	296-49-3438	Pay rate:	$1,750
Address:	175 Bunker Hill Lane, Huntington, CA 95394	Pay type:	Salary
Phone:	(707) 555-3856	Position:	Acct Sup
Date of Birth:	9/7/68	Filing Status:	Married
Date of Employment:	2/14/01	Withholding Allowances	3
Date of Last Raise:	2/16/03		

Name: José G. Rodriquez			
Social Security No:	124-11-7755	Pay rate:	$2,550
Address:	2953 Whistler Hill Lane, Huntington, CA 95394	Pay type:	Salary
Phone:	(707) 555-2024	Position:	Supervisor
Date of Birth:	7/7/71	Filing Status:	Married
Date of Employment:	11/3/93	Withholding Allowances	4
Date of Last Raise:	1/1/03		

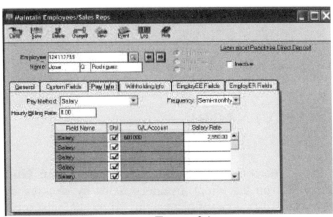

Figure 24

8. Click on the **Pay Info** tab to enter the employee type and pay rate information. The **Pay Method** for the hourly employees is "Hourly - Hours per Pay Period" and for salaried employees is "Salary." You will need to enter the Regular Hourly Rate and the Overtime Hourly Rate (1.5 times the regular hourly rate) for hourly employees. All employees are paid on the 15th and the last day of each month. Enter the withholding information on the **Withholding Info** tab. Make sure you save each employee as they are

entered. When you are finished entering the data for all four employees, click on **Close** and mark the task as completed.

9. Click on **Enter Your Employee Beginning Balances**, and enter the payroll information for each employee as of December 15, 2003. You will use the first column only and enter the following year-to-date information (**Hint: You will need to enter those amounts which represent deductions from gross pay as negative amounts.**)

Name	Gross Pay	Federal Income Tax	FICA Withheld	Medicare Withheld	Net Pay
Bryan, T	33,455.63	3,815.00	2,074.25	485.11	27,081.27
Hissom, R	31,750.78	4,110.00	1,968.55	460.39	25,211.84
Johnson, A	38,050.00	3,157.00	2,359.10	551.73	31,982.17
Rodriquez, J	58,650.00	5,543.00	3,636.30	850.43	48,620.27

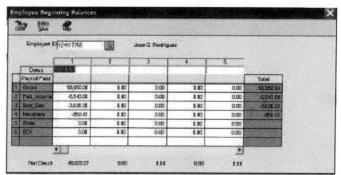

Figure 25

When you are finished entering the data for all four employees, click on **Close** and mark the task as completed.

10. If you wish, you may close the file at this time.

SETTING UP INVENTORY

Requirements
1. Open the Chateau Americana file. Click on **Setup Guide** and select **Inventory**. Set up the initial inventory fields by clicking on **Select Your Inventory Defaults**. Do not change any of the defaults under the **General** tab.

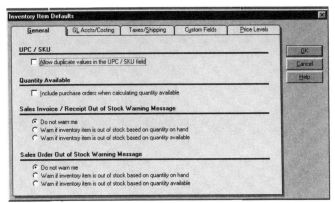

Figure 26

2. Click on the **GL Accts/Costing** tab. Set up the default accounts as follows: GL/Sales Inc should be set to Sales - 410000, GL Invtry/Wage should be set to Inventory – Finished Goods - 145000, and GL Cost Sales should be set to Cost of Goods Sold — 510000 (only for stock items). You will also need to set the GL Freight Account to Cost of Goods Sold - 510000. Leave the costing method as FIFO. Click **OK** and mark the task as completed. Do not modify settings on the other tabs.

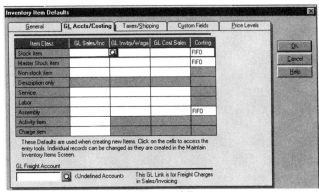

Figure 27

3. Click on **Set up Your Inventory Items**. On the **General** tab enter the following information for each inventory item: Item ID, Description, Price, Item Tax Type (select 2 - Exempt), and Last Unit Cost. Be sure to save after inputting each inventory item. Do not enter any information below the heavy black line at this time. Information regarding finished goods inventory is as follows:

Inventory ID	Description	Price	Last Unit Cost	Quantity On Hand	Beginning Balance
R130064	Cabernet Franc	$7.00	$4.50	5,964	$ 26,838.00
R130061	Cabernet Sauvignon	6.50	4.20	65,784	276,292.80
R130056	Merlot	6.00	4.62	83,484	385,696.08
R130072	Shiraz	6.25	4.58	75,888	347,567.04
W120080	Chardonnay	7.00	4.54	420,552	1,909,306.08
W120019	Chenin Blanc	5.25	3.34	44,532	148,736.88
W120015	Riesling	4.85	2.86	118,596	339,184.56

| W120016 | Sauvignon Blanc | 4.85 | 2.86 | 93,636 | $ 267,798.96 |
| S140000 | Sparkling Brut | 11.00 | 7.28 | 47,064 | 342,625.91 |

When you are finished entering all of the inventory items, click **Close** and mark the task as completed.

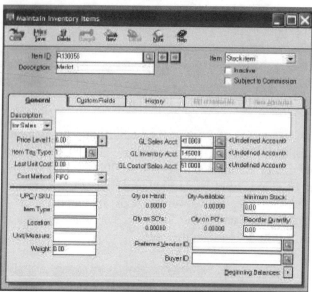

Figure 28

4. Click on **Enter Your Inventory Beginning Balances**. Enter the quantity on hand and the unit cost for each inventory item (last unit cost). When you are finished click **OK** and mark the task as completed.

5. The last item in the Setup Guide is Jobs. You do not need to enter information for this area.

6. If you wish, you may close the file at this time.

ENTERING TRANSACTIONS

Requirements

1. Open the Chateau Americana file. Click on **Navigation Aids**.

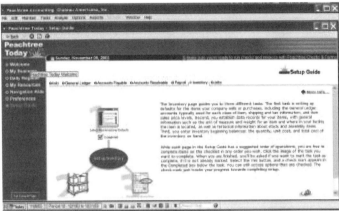

Figure 29

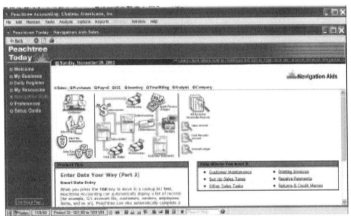

Figure 30

You can use the icons and menu bar in the **Navigation Aids** window to enter transactions and perform various maintenance activities (e.g., create new suppliers, customers, etc.). You can find the same selections on the **Tasks** menu bar at the top of the window.

2. Using the transactions listed below examine the first transaction for December 16. (Note: Documents supporting the transactions are provided behind the Year-End Procedures and Summary.) You will notice that it is a sale to California Premium Beverage. Enter this transaction in Peachtree by clicking on **Sales/Invoicing**.

Using the **View** button, select the customer name. Notice that the Customer ID number appears next to the **View** button and the customer name and address appear below. Enter the Invoice # and the transaction date and complete the remainder of the form. Do not enter the sales account representative since you have not set up these individuals as employees of the company. Do not enter any of the shippers for these transactions. Click **Save** after you have entered all information pertaining to the transaction.

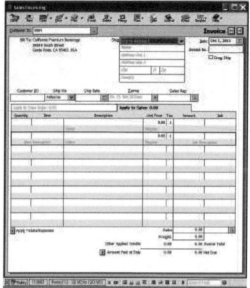

Figure 31

Notice that when you click on **Save** you get a warning telling you that the customer balance will exceed the credit limit. This occurs because you did not set up credit limits. This is a very useful internal control. We will, however, ignore this message for purposes of this assignment. Click **OK** and close the window.

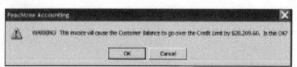

Figure 32

December	Transaction
16	Receive a purchase order from California Premium Beverage. Fill and ship the order. Complete Invoice No. 15535 and record the sale in the journals and ledgers (do not complete the "Sales Rep" field).
16	Order 18,000 lbs. white grapes at $1.05 per pound from Mendocino Vineyards. Complete Purchase Order No. 9682 (do not complete the "Item" field).
16	Purchase a 2002 Ford truck for $26,750.00. The terms include a $4,750.00 down payment and a 3-year, 6% promissory note to Ford Credit for the remaining $22,000.00. Principal and interest on the note are due monthly beginning January 4, 2004. The company expects the truck to have a useful life of 5 years and no salvage value. Prepare Check No. 19257 payable to Potter Valley Ford for the down payment and record the transaction in the journals and ledgers (do not complete the "Vendor ID" field).

17	Receive a phone complaint from Seaside Distributors about a case of Chenin Blanc that was damaged in shipment. The case was part of Invoice No. 15175, dated November 5, 2003, in the amount of $20,438.40. Seaside paid the invoice on November 19, 2003 and took advantage of the discount (terms 3/15, net 30). Prepare Credit Memo No. 2753 to write-off the damaged inventory that was not returned (do not complete the "Sales Rep" or "Item" fields), and prepare Check No. 19286 to reimburse Seaside for the damaged goods (do not complete the "Vendor ID" field).
19	Receive $850 dividend income from investment in Seagate shares. The cash receipt was included in Cash Receipts Summary No. 5712 which is not shown here. Record the cash receipt in the journals and ledgers (do not complete the "Customer ID" field).
19	Receive payment in full from Pacific Distribution Co. on Invoice No. 15243 dated November 13, 2003, in the amount of $19,576.80. The receipt was included in Cash Receipts Summary No. 5712 which is not shown here. Record the cash receipt in the journals and ledgers.
19	Receive a purchase order with payment from Ukiah Distributors. Fill and ship the order. The receipt was included in Cash Receipts Summary No. 5712 which is not shown here. Record the sale in the journals and ledgers (do no complete the "Customer ID" or "Sales Rep" fields).
22	Receive 14,000 lbs. red grapes at $0.99 per pound from Mendocino Vineyards. Also received Invoice No. M7634 from Mendocino Vineyards with the shipment. Terms on the invoice are 2/10, net 30. The receipt was included on Receiving Report No. 17251. Record the inventory in the journals and ledgers using the gross method (do not complete the "Item" field).
26	Receive utility bill from Pacific Gas and Electric in the amount of $18,887.62. Prepare Check No. 19402 and record the payment in the journals and ledgers.
30	Receive Brokerage Advice from Edwards Jones for purchase of 500 shares of Microsoft at $49.20 per share plus $400 broker's commission. Prepare Check No. 19468 and record the purchase in the journals and ledgers (do not complete the "Vendor ID" field).
31	Receive payment in full for the December 15 purchase from California Premium Beverage. The receipt was included in Cash Receipts Summary No. 5718 which is not shown here. Record the cash receipt in the journals and ledgers.
31	Prepare Check No. 19473 payable to Mendocino Vineyards for the shipment received on December 22 and record the payment in the journals and ledgers.
31	Prepare Payroll Checks (Nos. 7111-7114) for Anna Johnson, José Rodriguez, Tom Bryan, and Bob Hissom and record the payroll transactions in the journals and ledgers. Time cards for Tom and Bob are provided. Prepare Check No. 19474 to transfer cash from the general cash account to the payroll account (do not complete the "Vendor ID" field).

31	Prepare Check No. 19475 to repay $50,000 of the principal on long-term debt to Bank of Huntington and record the payment in the journals and ledgers (do not complete the "Vendor ID" field).

3. Continue working through the transactions listed above, selecting **Sales/Invoicing**, **Receipts**, **Purchases Orders**, **Payments** or **Payroll Entry**, as appropriate. Be sure the default accounts being used by the Peachtree Journals are the appropriate accounts for the particular transaction you are entering. You can check the accounts being debited and credited by each transaction by clicking on the **Journal** icon once you have entered the information needed at the top of the transaction screen. If necessary, you can then change the GL account. However, f the defaults have been set up properly, the Sales Journal will post to Sales and Accounts Receivable; the Cash Receipts Journal will post to Cash, Sales Discounts, and Accounts Receivable.

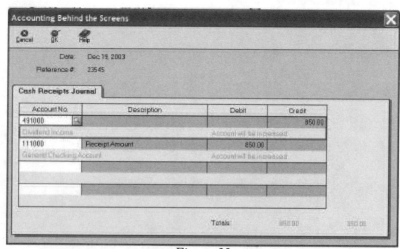

Figure 33

Remember that not all customers receive credit terms. For those customers who have remitted a check along with their order, you will need to use the **Receipts** task. If a customer number is not available, tab past the Customer ID field, enter the customer name and address, and enter the details of the sales transaction.

You will also use the **Receipts** task for other miscellaneous cash receipts.

Note that when you enter the payroll data the net pay is slightly different from the net pay you calculated if you prepared the payroll checks in the *CAST Manual AIS Module*. This is because Peachtree uses the Percentage Method for calculating federal income tax withheld whereas the *CAST Manual AIS Module* uses the Wage Bracket Method tables.

MONTH-END PROCEDURES

1. Calculate monthly accrued interest expense for the $22,000 installment note to Ford Credit (based on 365 days per year and interest starting to accrue on December 17, 2003). Make the appropriate adjusting entry. The payable is posted to Other Accrued Expenses Payable.

2. For your convenience, depreciation in the amount of $105,341.50 has been calculated on all assets for the month of December **except** for the Ford Pickup. Calculate the depreciation for the truck and add that amount to the $105,341.50 to determine the total depreciation expense for December. Record the appropriate adjusting entry in the General Journal.

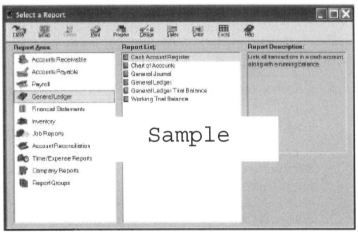

Figure 34

3. Your account balances can be verified at this time by clicking on **G/L – All General Ledger Reports** and selecting **Working Trial Balance**. The transactions for the Payroll Journal, Accounts Receivable, and Accounts Payable can also be verified through the **Reports** menu.

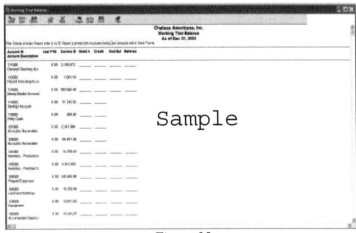

Figure 35

4. Take some time and examine some of the journals provided for you in Peachtree. If you completed the *CAST Manual AIS Module*, think about the similarities and differences of these journals to those you prepared manually. For example, compare and contrast the processes required to create and post a sales entry in Peachtree to those required in the *CAST Manual AIS Module*. You should observe that the defaults you created during set-up have simplified the posting process, but also have obscured part of the double-entry process.

YEAR-END PROCEDURES

1. Year-end adjusting entries should be recorded in the general journal after reconciling the unadjusted trial balance (the beginning balances in the working trial balance). **DO NOT** close the books for the end of the year. Prepare the following year-end adjusting journal entries:

   a. Calculate the allowance for bad debts using the net sales method. Experience indicates that 0.05% of net sales should be set aside for bad debts. Record the appropriate adjusting entry.

   b. The calculation of federal income tax expense is a year-end adjusting entry but it cannot be made until all other entries have been made and net income before taxes has been determined. Therefore, you must first calculate net income before taxes. Then calculate federal income tax expense and record the adjusting entry. (**HINT:** Use rates in effect as of January 2003.)

   Adjusting entries should be verified through the working trial balance as was done previously.

2. Print, and prepare to submit, the financial statements (including the **Balance Sheet**, the **Income Statement**, and the **Statement of Cash Flows**), the **Aged Receivables Report,** and the **Aged Payables Report**. (Note that there is no Fixed Assets Trial Balance.) These reports are accessed by clicking on **All General Ledger Reports** and then clicking on: (1) **Financial Statements** and selecting each of the financial statements to be printed; (2) **Accounts Receivable** and selecting Aged Receivables; or (3) **Accounts Payable** and selecting Aged Payables.

California Premium Beverage

PURCHASE ORDER

39848 South Street
Santa Rosa, CA 95402
Phone (707) 555-7451 Fax (707) 555-7452

To:
Chateau Americana
3003 Vineyard Way
Huntington, CA 95394

Ship To:
California Premium Beverage
39848 South Street
Santa Rosa, CA 95402

ABC Permit #: A59782

P.O. DATE	P.O. NUMBER	SHIPPED VIA	F.O.B. POINT	TERMS
12/13/03	8746	CA Express	Destination	3/15, net 30

ITEM NO	QTY	SIZE	DESCRIPTION	UNIT PRICE	TOTAL
W120015	1512	0.750	Riesling	4.85	7,333.20
W120016	504	0.750	Sauvignon Blanc	4.85	2,444.40
W120019	336	0.750	Chenin Blanc	5.25	1,764.00
R130061	1176	0.750	Cabernet Sauvignon	6.50	7,644.00
R130056	672	0.750	Merlot	6.00	4,032.00
S140000	240	0.750	Sparkling Brut	11.00	2,640.00
W120080	336	0.750	Chardonnay	7.00	2,352.00
				TOTAL	28,209.60

Jorge Gonzalez   *12/13/03*
Authorized by   Date

Seagate Technology
Disc Drive
Scotts Valley, CA 95067

Lone Star Bank
Dallas, TX 27540

23545

Date ___ 12/15/03 ___

PAY ___ Eight Hundred Fifty and 00/100 Dollars -- $ ___ 850.00 ___

To the
order of

Chateau Americana
3003 Vineyard Way
Huntington, CA 95394

- SAMPLE, DO NOT CASH -

|:000000|: :000000000: 23545

Seagate Technology

23545

Reference	Amount
Dividend (850 Seagate Technology common shares @ $1.00)	$850.00

Pacific Distribution Company
10034 Westborough Boulevard
San Francisco, CA 94080

Bank of America
San Francisco, CA 94104

69712

Date ___12/16/03___

PAY___ Nineteen Thousand Five Hundred Seventy Six and 80/100 Dollars ------------------ $ ___19,576.80___

To The
Order Of

Chateau Americana
3003 Vineyard Way
Huntington, CA 95394

- SAMPLE, DO NOT CASH -

⑊:000000⑊: :000000000: 69712

Pacific Distribution Company

69712

Reference	Net Amount
Invoice #15243, customer # 0505	$19,576.80

PURCHASE ORDER

PO Number: 4376
Date: 12/19/03

To:
Chateau Americana
3003 Vineyard Way
Huntington, CA 95394

Ship To:
Ukiah Distributors
3224 Greenlawn Street
Ukiah, CA 95482
Phone (707) 555-1705 Fax (707) 555-1706

SHIPPED VIA	ABC #	F.O.B. POINT	TERMS
United Express	A557912	Huntington	

ITEM NO	QTY	SIZE	DESCRIPTION	UNIT PRICE	TOTAL
W120015	480	0.750	Riesling	4.85	2,328.00
W120080	468	0.750	Chardonnay	7.00	3,276.00
W120019	300	0.750	Chenin Blanc	5.25	1,575.00
R130072	780	0.750	Shiraz	6.25	4,875.00
R130056	672	0.750	Merlot	6.00	4,032.00
				TOTAL	16,086.00

Chrystal Harrington   *12/19/03*
_____   _____
Authorized by   Date

Ukiah Distributors				17003
3224 Greenlawn Street		Humboldt Bank		
Ukiah, CA 95482		Ukiah, CA 95482		
			Date	12/19/03

PAY___ Sixteen Thousand Eighty Six and 00/100 Dollars -------------------------------------- $ ___ 16,086.00 ___

To the
order of

Chateau Americana
3003 Vineyard Way
Huntington, CA 95394

- SAMPLE, DO NOT CASH -

¦:000000¦: :000000000: 17003

Ukiah Distributors		17003
Reference	Discount	Net Amount
Payment for PO 4376		$16,086.00

CUSTOMER INVOICE

Invoice Number **M7634**

Mendocino Vineyards
8654 Witherspoon Way
Hopland, CA 95449
Phone: (707) 555-1890

Invoice Date 12/20/2003

Sold To:	Ship To:
Chateau Americana, Inc. 3003 Vineyard Way Huntington, CA 95394	Chateau Americana, Inc. 3003 Vineyard Way Huntington, CA 95394
Credit Terms: 2/10, Net 30	

	Customer I.D	Customer P.O. Number
	CHATAM	9660

Description	Product Number	Quantity	Cost	Extended
Cabernet Sauvignon Grapes	CS1250	14,000 lbs.	$0.99	$13,860.00

Total Cost: $13,860.00

Comments:

Payment Coupon

Bill Date: 12/23/2003

Please Pay by 01/17/2004
$18,887.62

Amount Enclosed

Account No. 21790-1879

Chateau Americana, Inc.
3003 Vineyard Way
Huntington, CA 95394

Send Payment to:

Pacific Gas and Electric
P.O. Box 2575
San Francisco, CA 94103

- -

Retain bottom portion for your records, detach and return stub with payment.

Service For:	Chateau Americana, Inc. 3003 Vineyard Way Huntington, CA 95394	Your Account Number **21790-1879**	Rate Class **Commercial**	Billing Date **12/23/2003**

Meter Number	Service Period	Days	Type of Reading	Multiplier	Units	Meter Readings Current	Past	Usage
68869800	11/23/03 – 12/23/03	31	Actual	1	KWH	1098412	1001301	97111

Previous Balance		16,895.53
Payment		16,895.53
Balance Forward		0.00
Current Charges		18,887.62

	Due Date	Total Due
	01/17/2004	18,887.62

Pacific Gas and Electric
1000 Energy Drive, San Francisco, CA 94103, (415) 973-8943

Edward Jones Financial Services
100 Market Street
San Francisco, CA 94109
(415)504-9000

Customer
Chateau Americana, Inc.
3003 Vineyard Way
Huntington, CA 95394

Account Number
02334-85763

Tax Identification #
23-7788954

SAVE THIS STATEMENT FOR TAX PURPOSES

Date	Description	Symbol	Fees and/or Commissions($)	Net Dollar Amount ($)	Share Price ($)	Transaction Shares
12/30/03	Microsoft Corporation Common Shares	MSFT	400.00	24,600.00	49.20	500.0000

California Premium Beverage
39848 South Street
Santa Rosa, CA 95402

Bay View Bank
Santa Rosa, CA 95407

21803

Date ___12/29/03___

PAY ___Twenty Seven Thousand Three Hundred Sixty Three and 31/100 Dollars ----------------- $ ___27,363.31___

To The
Order Of

Chateau Americana
3003 Vineyard Way
Huntington, CA 95394

- SAMPLE, DO NOT CASH -

⑈000000⑈ ⑆000000000⑆ 21803

California Premium Beverage

21803

Reference	Discount	Net Amount
# 0504 Invoice 15535	846.29	$27,363.31

Period Ending: December 31, 2003
Employee Name: Thomas P. Bryan
Signature: Tom Bryan
Approved: PJB

	7th Day	6th Day	5th Day	4th Day	3rd Day	2nd Day	1st Day
Out			04:02 PM	04:33 PM	05:00 PM		
In			11:58 AM	11:59 AM	12:01 PM		
Out			11:30 AM	11:30 AM	11:30 AM		
In			06:45 AM	07:31 AM	07:29 AM		
Approved			4	4.75	4.5	4	5 / 4

Period Ending: December 26, 2003
Employee Name: Thomas P. Bryan
Signature: Tom Bryan
Approved: PJB

	7th Day	6th Day	5th Day	4th Day	3rd Day	2nd Day	1st Day
Out		Holiday	Holiday	04:00 PM	04:00 PM	04:04 PM	
In				12:02 PM	12:01 PM	12:02 PM	
Out				11:30 AM	11:33 AM	11:31 AM	
In				07:29 AM	07:30 AM	07:28 AM	
Approved	4	4	4	4	4	4	4 / 4 / 4

Period Ending: December 19, 2003
Employee Name: Thomas P. Bryan
Signature: Tom Bryan
Approved: PJB

	7th Day	6th Day	5th Day	4th Day	3rd Day	2nd Day	1st Day
Out	04:00 PM	04:01 PM	04:02 PM	04:03 PM			
In	12:01 PM	12:00 PM	11:58 AM	11:59 AM			
Out	11:30 AM	11:30 AM	11:30 AM	11:30 AM			
In	07:29 AM	07:31 AM	07:30 AM	07:31 AM			
Approved	4	4	4	4	4	4	4 / 4

Time Card — December 31, 2003

Period Ending	December 31, 2003
Employee Name	Robert T. Hissom
Signature	*Bob Hissom*
Approved	*PJB*

Day	In	Out	In	Out	Approved
1st Day					
2nd Day	07:26 AM	11:30 AM	11:55 AM	03:57 PM	4
3rd Day	07:30 AM	11:30 AM	11:59 AM	04:01 PM	4
4th Day	07:32 AM	11:32 AM	11:58 AM	04:00 PM	4
5th Day					
6th Day					
7th Day					

Time Card — December 26, 2003

Period Ending	December 26, 2003
Employee Name	Robert T. Hissom
Signature	*Bob Hissom*
Approved	*PJB*

Day	In	Out	In	Out	Approved
1st Day					
2nd Day	07:31 AM	11:31 AM	12:01 PM	04:03 PM	4
3rd Day	07:30 AM	11:33 AM	12:00 PM	04:00 PM	4
4th Day	07:29 AM	11:30 AM	12:04 PM	04:03 PM	4
5th Day	*Holiday*				4
6th Day	*Holiday*				4
7th Day					4

Time Card — December 19, 2003

Period Ending	December 19, 2003
Employee Name	Robert T. Hissom
Signature	*Bob Hissom*
Approved	*PJB*

Day	In	Out	In	Out	Approved
1st Day					
2nd Day					
3rd Day	07:30 AM	11:34 AM	12:02 PM	04:03 PM	4
4th Day	07:31 AM	11:30 AM	11:59 AM	04:00 PM	4
5th Day	07:27 AM	11:30 AM	12:02 PM	03:59 PM	4
6th Day	07:29 AM	11:30 AM	12:01 PM	04:02 PM	4
7th Day					

DATABASE APPLICATIONS
USING MICROSOFT® ACCESS 2002:
The Winery at Chateau Americana

LEARNING OBJECTIVES

After completing and discussing this material, you should be able to:

- Recognize and explain the purpose of the elements of a relational database
- Build selected elements of a database management system
- Recognize and evaluate the strengths and weaknesses of the controls embedded in a database management system
- Compare and contrast a database package with a general ledger package and with a manual accounting information system

BACKGROUND

Before you begin the database assignments, it is important to understand a little about a database management system and its terminology and to understand the scope of these assignments. A database management system (DBMS) is based on a logical data model. The majority of DBMSs in existence today (*Access, MySQL, Oracle, FoxPro*, etc.) are based on the relational data model. A relational database (which will be the only type of database to which we refer) represents all of the data about the entity in a collection of tables. The following exercises are specific to *Microsoft® Access 2002*, but the theory discussed herein applies to any relational database.

The structures and methods used to manage the data are called objects. There are seven types of objects in *Access*. They are tables, queries, forms, reports, pages, macros, and modules.

Tables are the fundamental storage entity of a relational database. Therefore, all database data is stored in one or more tables comprised of rows and columns. A row, or **record**, contains all the data about a specific instance, or item, in the table.

A column, or **field**, in a table represents characteristics or attributes of the data. Most tables will contain one field that represents the **primary key** (i.e., a value that uniquely identifies each record). In *Figure 1* below, CustomerNo is the primary key. Each field can contain only one data type. Data types constrain the type of data that can be entered into a field (e.g., text, number, counter, currency, date/time).

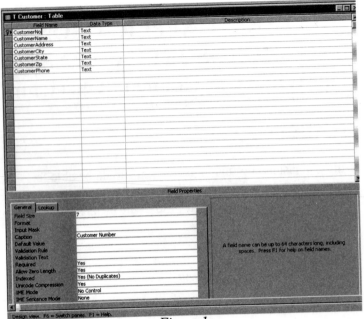

Figure 1

A record's fields contain individual values for each attribute that characterizes that particular record, as shown in *Table 1*.

CustomerNo	CustomerName	CustomerAddress	CustomerCity
WD564	Wine Distributors, Inc.	1285 Napa Ave.	Mendocino

Table 1

Queries are used for asking questions about the data in one or more tables in a database. Queries can be used to locate and display a subset of the records of a table (the **select query**), modify data (using one of four types of **action queries**) such as combining information from several tables into a single result (the **append query**), or perform calculations on fields, or specify criteria for searching the data (the **parameter query**).

Queries can be created in *Access* using SQL (structured query language), a text-based query language. Syntax is very important and very specific in creating SQL statements. The SQL in *Figure 2* uses a field (SupplierNo) common to two tables that might exist in an organization's database (i.e., a Purchase Order table and a Supplier table) to present several fields from the two tables in one form.

Queries can also be created in *Access* using QBE (query by example), a graphical query language in which the user selects one or more tables to query and then selects the columns which should be included in the query response. Because of its graphical interface, QBE is typically the technique of choice because it is easier to use. QBE allows the user to place values or expressions, called selection criteria, below particular field names, thereby limiting the records that are retrieved. Thus, queries are used to reduce the amount of displayed information, summarizing it, and giving it meaning. *Figure 3* presents the same query using the QBE technique as was described in *Figure 2*.

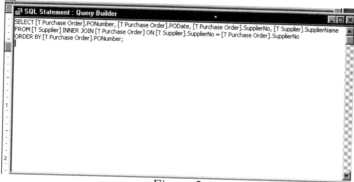

Figure 2

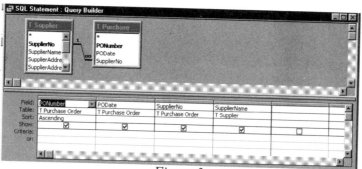

Figure 3

Forms allow the user to see data from tables in a more convenient format. Forms can be customized so that they precisely match an existing paper form, making it easier to move from hard copy to soft copy. Forms contain **labels** and **controls**. **Controls** display data, perform actions, or make forms easier to read. Text boxes are examples of bound controls. A bound control is one that obtains its data from a field in an underlying table or query. An unbound control is not connected to a field. Lines, shapes, and instructions regarding the use of a form are examples of unbound controls. **Labels** can be attached to controls, in which case they are pre-specified by the **Caption**, or they can be stand-alone, in which case they are created using the **Label** icon in the Toolbox. Both of these will be discussed later). Forms can also include other forms, or subforms, to allow data entry into more than one table at a time.

Embedded aids and prompts are other useful tools that aid in the creation of forms. Some of these can be created by the database designer and some of them are provided by the program itself. For example, **Form Navigation** buttons, located at the bottom of the screen, enable the user to move to another record by moving up or down one record at a time, selecting a particular record number, or moving to the first or last record in the table.

Reports utilize data from one table or several tables linked together to provide the user with meaningful information. Reports can be used to sort, group, and summarize data in almost limitless ways. As a result, reports can appear as invoices, purchase orders, sales summaries, or financial statements. However, whereas the user can enter, edit, and interact with the data in a **Form**, he or she can not interact with the data in a **Report**.

Pages, or data access pages, are similar to forms. They also have the benefit of being able to accommodate live data from the Internet or an intranet outside of an Access database.

Macros are more advanced *Access* objects. They contain sets of instructions that automate frequently performed tasks, such as opening a form, printing a report, or processing an order. They can also assist in the creation of turnkey applications that anyone can use, whether or not they have experience with *Access*.

Modules are even more advanced *Access* objects than macros. They are similar to macros in that they allow for automation and customization. However, these tools require knowledge of *Visual Basic* programming and give the user more precise control over the actions taken.

REQUIREMENTS

These assignments will be limited to familiarizing you with tables, queries, forms, and reports. The objective of this assignment is not to provide you with expertise in the development of a database, but to provide you with an initiation in and an appreciation of both the complexity and the power of a database when used to create an accounting information system.

Good programming procedures require a certain amount of standardization. For example, when saving tables, queries, forms, and reports created in a database, it is often useful to use a naming convention (i.e., a method which names the objects in a way that will let the user know to which classification the object belongs). Therefore, the naming convention indicated in *Table 2* will be used throughout this assignment:

Table	T *tablename*
Queries	Q *queryname*
Forms	F *formname*
Reports	R *reportname*

Table 2

Please read the following sections carefully. They are intended to be tutorial in nature as well as providing you with the information necessary to complete your *Access* assignments. In some instances, the assignment provides you with explicit instructions about creating the necessary tables, forms, queries and reports. However, in other instances, the assignment allows you to make choices about design considerations such as form style, size, font size, etc. Therefore, it is imperative to follow the directions carefully **AND** to critique the forms and reports you create from a user's perspective.

Note: Words or characters that you are asked to type are commonly displayed in bold with quotation marks. The quotation marks should not be typed unless otherwise specified.

Finally, as always, it is important to **back your work up frequently**!

CREATING A NEW DATABASE AND NEW TABLE

Requirements

1. Create a new database by launching *Access*. On the right hand side of your screen, click on **Blank Database** under **New**.

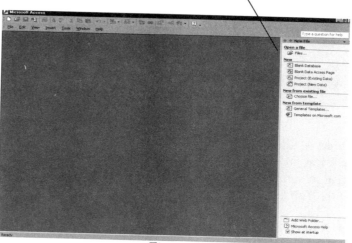

Figure 4

Notice that you are now prompted to name the new database (the default name is "db1"). Check with your instructor to determine the appropriate file naming convention.

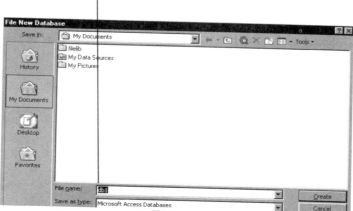

Figure 5

After you have entered the appropriate file name click **Create**. The file is automatically created. You are now ready to design the database. As discussed previously, tables are the fundamental storage entity of a relational database so we will begin there.

2. Using your newly created database, generate a table for your database. Select the **Tables** tab in the **Database** window. Click on the **Design** icon or click on **Create table in Design view**. See *Figure 6.*

Figure 6

A **Table** window is displayed which contains three columns: **Field Name, Data Type,** and **Description.** You may move among these columns by either clicking in various fields with the mouse or by clicking in a field and then using the **Tab** key.

Field Names can be up to 64 characters and can include almost any combination of letters, numbers, spaces, and special characters. **Field Names** may not include a period, an exclamation point, a backquote character, or brackets. In addition, a **Field Name** cannot contain leading spaces. When the cursor is in the **Data Type** column, you will see a button to pull down a menu. This button allows you to select the **Data Type** for the given **Field Name**. Take some time to explore the various data types. The **Description** property is optional and is used to provide useful information about the table or query and its fields. Check with your instructor to determine whether you are to complete the description field for this assignment.

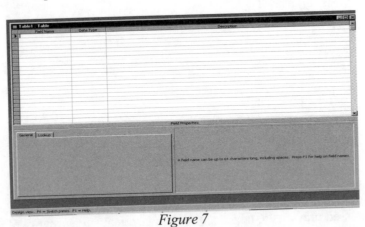

Figure 7

3. Type "**SupplierNo**" in the first Field Name space.

*At this point, it is very important that you check your work. Before you tab out of the Field Name, make it a habit to check your spelling. Field Names are recorded in the **data dictionary**. The data dictionary contains information about the entire structure of the database. Thus, for each data element, the data dictionary might include the data element name, its description, the records in which it is contained, its source, its field* *length and type, the program in which it is used, the outputs in which it is contained, and its authorized users.*

It is often very difficult to remove data elements from the data dictionary. Therefore, it is critical that you check your work very carefully when you are creating fields in tables.

4. Once you have verified the field name, press **Enter** or the **Tab** key. Make **SupplierNo** the primary key by clicking the **Primary Key** icon.

   As we discussed earlier, a primary key is a value that uniquely identifies each record. By defining a primary key, Access does three things:
   a. It insures that no two records in that table will have the same value in the primary key field.
   b. It keeps records sorted according to the primary key field.
   c. It speeds up processing.

5. Set its data type to **Text** since Chateau Americana uses a combination of letters and numbers to identify their suppliers.

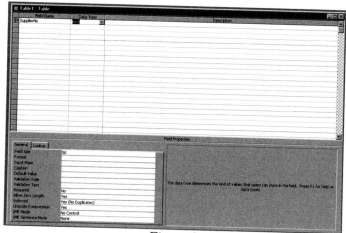

Figure 8

When you move from the **Field Name** column to the **Data Type** column, a **Field Properties** pane is displayed at the bottom of the screen. You can toggle to the **Field Properties** pane by pressing **F6** or you can move to the **Field Properties** pane by moving your mouse to the desired field. This pane allows the user to specify the properties for the chosen field and type. *Table 3* describes the most important field properties.

Field Property	Description
Field Size	Sets the maximum size for data stored in a Text, Number or AutoNumber field. In a text field the default size is 50, but size may range from 1 to 255. In Number fields, the default is set to Long Integer.
Format	Specifies how data is to be displayed in a field. It is particularly useful in specifying the format for numbers, currency, dates, and times.
Decimal Places	Specifies the number of digits to the right of the decimal point. "**Auto**" allows the Format property to determine the number of decimal places automatically.
Input Mask	Makes data entry easier by adjusting the data entered so that it conforms to the standard set in the Input Mask. It is also used to control the values users can enter.
Caption	Specifies the text for labels attached to controls created by dragging a field from the field list and serves as the heading for the field when the table or query is in Datasheet view.
Default Value	Specifies a default value for a field (e.g., Napa can be set as the Default Value for a City field; the user then has the option of accepting the Default Value or inputting different data).
Validation Rule	Specifies the requirements for data entry. For example, you can create a rule that specifies that all entries must contain five numeric characters as might be the case with zip codes.
Validation Text	Text input in the Validation Text property specifies the message to be displayed to the user when the Validation Rule is violated. For example, when a record is added for a new employee, you can require that the entry in the **Start Date** field fall between the company's founding date and the current date. If the date entered is not in this range, you can display a message such as, "**Start date is incorrect**."
Required	Specifies whether or not a value is required in a field. If **Yes**, the field requires a value. If **No**, no entry is required.
Allow Zero Length	Indicates whether an empty string (i.e., a string containing no characters) is a valid entry. If **Yes**, the field will accept an empty string even when the Required property is set to **Yes**.
Indexed	Sets a single-field index (i.e., a feature which speeds the sorting and searching of a table). The primary key is always indexed. When a record is indexed, it is also necessary to specify whether duplicates will be allowed. For example, when creating a purchase order table, the primary key might be "PO #" and you would not want to allow duplicates. However, when creating a table to add the inventory purchased on a particular purchase order, you might still want to be able to sort and search based upon the PO # (which would require that field to be indexed), but you would expect that a particular purchase order might have several items of inventory. Therefore, duplicates would be allowed.

Table 3

6. Press **F6** to switch to the **Field Properties** pane of the **Table** window and establish the following properties for **SupplierNo** (No entries are required for other properties for **SupplierNo.**):

Field Size	5
Caption	**Supplier Number**
Validation Rule	**Like "?####"** (Note: Include quotation marks)
Validation Text	**Invalid entry. The Supplier Number must consist of two letters and three numbers.**
Required	**Yes**
Indexed	**Yes (No duplicates)**

Table 4

7. All Data Types for all subsequent fields in this table should be set to **Text**. The second Field Name should be **SupplierName**, the Field Size is **35**, and the Caption should be **Supplier Name**. The third Field Name should be **SupplierAddress1**, the Field Size is **35**, and the Caption should be **Supplier Address**. The fourth Field Name should be **SupplierAddress2** and the field size is **35**. There is no caption for this field. The fifth Field Name should be **SupplierCity** with a Field Size of **25** and an appropriate Caption.

8. The sixth Field Name should be **SupplierState**. The Field Size is **2**. Set the Input Mask property for the **SupplierState** field by typing ">LL," and use an appropriate Caption.

9. The seventh Field Name should be **SupplierZip**. Set the Field Size to **10** and use an appropriate Caption. Activate the **Input Mask Wizard** (the button with three small dots located in the Input Mask Property) to aid in making a template for the Zip Code. You will have to save the table before proceeding. Save the table as **T Supplier** (Remember the naming convention discussed earlier). Select **Zip Code** from the menu, click **Next** twice, and choose to store the Zip Code with the hyphen. See *Figure 9*. Click on **Finish.**

10. The last field name is **SupplierTelephone**. Set the Field Size to **14** and use an appropriate Caption. Use the Input Mask Wizard to set the Input Mask property to the pre-defined Phone Number setting.

11. You are now finished with the table. When you close this object and all objects in the future, use the **X** in the upper right hand corner of the screen to save and close the object. By doing this, you will avoid having to provide names to queries that are underlying the database that should not appear in the Query window, thus limiting the possibility that users may gain unauthorized access.

12. If you wish to quit *Access* at this time, simply close the program and your database will be saved with the name you used to create it.

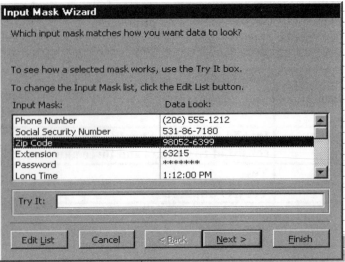

Figure 9

CREATING A FORM

Although data can be entered from the datasheet view of a table, the utilization of forms makes data entry easier and the database more user friendly. A form can display data in almost any format. A very simple form can be designed to display one record at a time. More complex forms can be created as 'fill-in-the-blanks' forms that resemble paper documents used within a company.

Requirements
1. Open your database. You will now enter relevant data into the Supplier Table (i.e., T Supplier) after you create a form utilizing the **Form Wizard**.

Figure 10

2. Select the **Forms** tab in your **Database** window and double click on the **Design** icon. Be sure that **T Supplier** is highlighted in the **Tables/Queries** box.

3. Select all the fields you created in the table for inclusion in the new form by clicking on the >> button in the middle of the window and click on **Next**. See *Figure 11*.

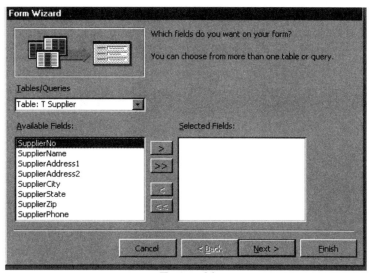

Figure 11

4. The next window allows you to choose a layout. Take some time to view each of the various layouts and then select the **Columnar** format. Click **Next**.

5. You are now presented with a selection of styles or backgrounds from which to choose. Again take some time to view each of the styles. Keep your users in mind when you choose a style and pick one that will be pleasing to the users. Click **Next**.

6. Recalling the naming convention discussed earlier, entitle the form **F Supplier**. Select **Modify the form's design.** Click **Finish.**

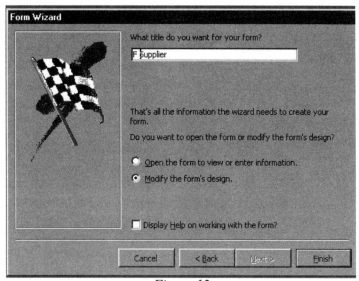

Figure 12

7. To enlarge the form's work area, place the mouse on the right side of the work area (i.e., the area that shows the background of the style you chose for your form) until the crosshairs appear. Click and drag the mouse to the right enlarging the work area approximately one to two inches. Similarly, add space for a form title by placing the mouse between the **Form Header** bar and the **Detail** bar until the crosshairs appear. Click and drag the **Detail** bar down approximately one-half inch.

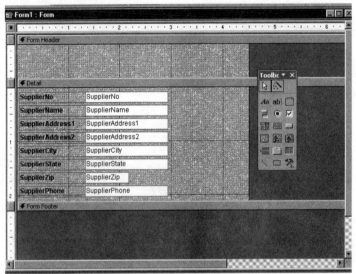

Figure 13

8. Click the **Label** icon on the **Toolbox** toolbar and then click in the form header area to create a stand-alone label for inclusion in the **Header** window. Type the label "**Supplier Form**." Click outside the label once and then click the label once again. Notice that the **Formatting** toolbar is enabled. Format the label using a **bold font of your choosing with a font size of 18**. Adjust the label text box as needed to properly display the label. Close the form and select **Yes** to save it.

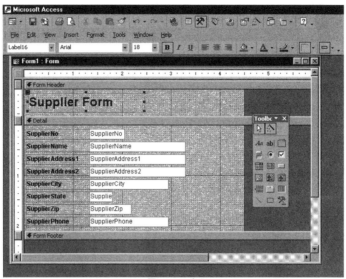

Figure 14

9. Now you are ready to begin entering data using your newly created Supplier form. Open the Supplier Form by double clicking on **F Supplier** in the **Database** window. Enter data for each of Chateau Americana's suppliers listed below:

Vendor Name	Vendor Number	Vendor Address	Vendor Phone
Delicio Vineyards	P2538	12701 South Fernwood Livermore, CA 94550	(925)555-1890
Mendocino Vineyards	P0652	8654 Witherspoon Way Hopland, CA 95449	(707)555-1890

As you enter the supplier information, pay attention to the size of the fields. You can adjust the size by clicking on the **Design View** and stretching or shrinking the field and then toggling back to the form by clicking on the **Form View** icon. After you have entered the first supplier's information press the **Enter** key to input the next supplier's information.

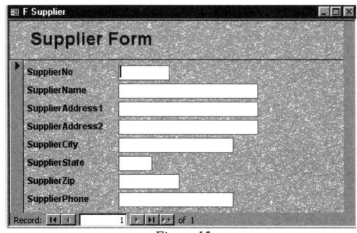

Figure 15

10. Close the form by clicking on the **X** in the upper right hand corner of the form.

11. If you wish to quit *Access* at this time, simply close the program and your database will be saved with the name you used to create it.

ENSURING SEQUENTIAL INTEGRITY

Completeness is an important aspect of internal control. Completeness suggests not only that all data in a transaction are captured, but also that all transactions are recorded. Therefore, it is important to ensure that no documents are lost or misplaced. One way to accomplish this is to pre-number documents and verify the sequential integrity of the completed documents.

Requirements
1. Open your *Access* database used for the previous assignments and create a new table.

2. The first Field Name in this new table is **PONumber**. Choose **AutoNumber** as the Data Type and enter **PO #** as the Caption. Do not change any other default values for this or other Field Names in the **Field Properties** pane unless instructed to do so.

3. The second Field Name is **PODate**. The Data type is **Date/Time**. Use the Input Mask Wizard to create the Input Mask property. You will have to save the table before proceeding. Save the table as **T Purchase Order**. *NOTE: A primary key is not to be designated at this time. When asked if a primary key should be created, click NO. You will set the primary key later.* Choose **Short Date** for the Input Mask. Click on **Next** twice and then click **Finish**. The Caption should be **PO Date**.

4. The third Field Name is **SupplierNo**. The Data Type should be set to **Text**. Set the Field Size to **5** and enter the Caption as **Supplier Number**. Close the **T Purchase Order** table.

   *Notice that you have already used the Field Name "SupplierNo." It was the primary key in the T Supplier table. When a field name appears in one table that is a primary key in another table, it is called a **Foreign Key**. Foreign keys are used to link tables together.*

5. Create a new table.

6. The only field in this table is **PONumber**. The Data Type should be **Number** and the Field Size property should be set to **Long Integer**.

7. Save the table as **T TempPONo**. When asked if a primary key should be created, click **NO**.

8. Open **T TempPONo** by double clicking the table name in the **Database** window. Click on the **Data Sheet** 🖩 view icon and then set the value of the **PONumber** to **9681**. Close the table.

9. Select the **Queries** tab in the **Database** window and click on **New** and then select **Design View** 🖾.

10. Double click on **T TempPONo** from the **Show Table** dialogue window and close the dialogue window.

11. From the menu bar click on the **Query Type** 🖽 pull-down menu and select **Append Query** ✚.

12. The **Append Query** copies some or all of the records from one table (e.g., the **T TempPONo**) to another table (e.g., the **T Purchase Order**). To begin the prenumbering of the purchase orders with 9682, the number you just entered in the **T TempPONo** table must be appended to the **T Purchase Order** table. To do this, select **T Purchase Order** in the **Table Name** pull-down menu in the **Append** window. Be sure that **Current Database** is selected and click **OK**.

13. In the **Append Query** window click on the first Field name cell and then click on the Field name button for the pull-down menu to select **PONumber**. Now, click on the **Run** 🗓 icon from the menu bar.

14. A dialog window will appear stating that one row will be appended. Click on **Yes** to append the row. Close and save the query as **Q PONumber.**

15. Open **T Purchase Order** in the Design view and designate **PONumber** as the primary key. Close and save the table. Finally, delete **T TempPONo**.

16. If you wish to quit *Access* at this time, simply close the program and your database will be saved with the name you used to create it.

CREATING RELATIONS

As stated previously, *Access* is a relational database. This implies that associations or relationships are created between common fields (i.e., columns) in two tables to link the data from one table to another. For example, one-to-one (1:1) relationships occur when a record (i.e., row) in a table relates to a record in another table once and only once. One-to-many (1:N) relationships occur when a record in a table relates to several records in another table. Many-to-many (N:N) relationships occur when several records in a table relate to several records in another table.

For example, there should be a one-to-many relationship established between the **Supplier** table and the **Purchase Order** table so that data regarding suppliers does not have to be duplicated on the purchase orders. In this section, you will set up these other tables for the expenditure cycle and create relations among them. The following instructions will aid in setting up a relationship linking the **Purchase Order** table to the **Supplier** table.

Requirements

1. Open your previously created database. Click on the **Relationships** icon, or select **Relationships** from the **Tools** menu.

2. In the **Relationships** window **Add** both the **T Supplier** and **T Purchase Order**. Close the **Show Table** dialogue window.

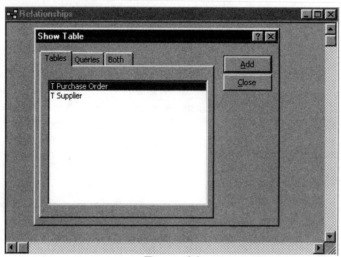

Figure 16

3. Click and drag the **SupplierNo** field in **T Supplier** to the **SupplierNo** field in the **T Purchase Order**.

4. Click the **Enforce Referential Integrity** check box. Referential integrity ensures that records referenced by a foreign key cannot be deleted unless the record containing the foreign key is first removed. Thus, in this case, a supplier cannot be deleted from the database if there is an outstanding purchase order for that supplier.

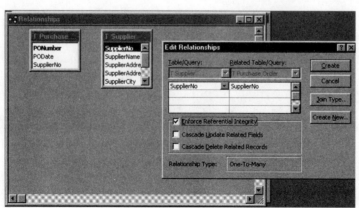

Figure 17

5. Click on the **Create** button.

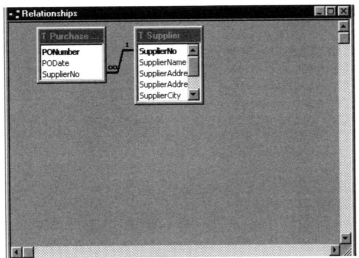

Figure 18

6. Save and close the relationship.

7. If you wish to quit *Access* at this time, simply close the program and your database will be saved with the name you used to create it.

INTEGRATING FORMS WITHIN FORMS

There are times when you may want to show data from tables that are linked with a one-to-many relationship. To do this, we can insert one form within another. That is, we can create a subform within the main form. For example, we might want to insert inventory data into a purchase order form. The following instructions will assist you in doing this.

Requirements

1. Open your *Access* database used for the previous assignments and create a new table.

2. The first Field Name is **InvCode**. Set the Data Type to **Text** and the Field Size to **7.** Enter the Caption as **Inventory Code**. Set this field as the table's primary key. Do not change any other default values for this or other Field Names in the **Field Properties** pane unless instructed to do so.

3. The second Field Name is **InvDescription**. Set Data Type to **Text**, the Field Size to **35**, and enter the Caption as **Description**.

4. The third Field Name is **InvCost**. Set Data Type to **Currency** and enter the Caption as **Cost.**

5. Save the table as **T Inventory** and close the table.

6. Create a new form with the **Form Wizard**.

7. Choose **T Inventory** from the combo box list in the **Form Wizard** dialogue window.

8. Select all of the available fields from **T Inventory** for inclusion in your new form. Click on **Next**. Choose a **Tabular** format and click on **Next**. Now, choose a backdrop for the form and click on **Next**. The form's title should be **F Inventory**. Be sure to select the radio button that allows you to modify the form design. Click on **Finish**.

9. Enlarge the **Form Header** section to create room for the heading. Drag the subheadings in the **Form Header** section lower to allow sufficient room for the form's heading. Click the **Label** icon on the **Toolbox** toolbar and then click in the form header area to create a stand-alone label for inclusion in the **Header** window Type the label "**Inventory.**" Set the font size for the label to an appropriate size.

10. Left align the label for **Cost** and drag it and its corresponding control box to the right to make more room for the **Description** field. Shrink the width of the label and the control box since these are more than wide enough for any potential entries. Widen the **Description** control box to allow for longer descriptions.

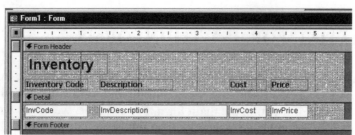

Figure 19

11. Review *Figure 19*. Notice that there is little empty space below the control boxes in the **Detail** section and the **Form Footer**. This is because the **Detail** section represents one record. Therefore, any space that is left in the **Detail** section will be included as space between each record (i.e., space between each line of inventory in our Inventory form).

12. Close and save the form. Open the **Inventory Form** and enter all inventory data from Chateau Americana's Inventory Price List found below. Close the form after all data is entered.

Inventory Code	Description	Cost
CK30110	1 ¾ US Cork	0.25
CK30120	2 US Cork	0.34
CP30130	Crème Caps Wine	0.11
CP30140	Black Caps Wine	0.09

BT30010	750 Green Bottle	0.47
BT30020	750 Brown Bottle	0.44
LB30210	Crème Wine Bottle Labels	0.18
RG10005	Red Grapes	1.10
WG20004	White Grapes	1.05

13. Now you need to create the table that will store the inventory data so that it can be inserted into the **Purchase Order** table. Create a new table.

14. The first Field Name is **PONumber**. Set the field's Data Type to **AutoNumber**. Enter the Caption as **PO #**. Set the Indexed property to **Yes (Duplicates OK)**. Do not change any other default values for this or other Field Names in the **Field Properties** pane unless instructed to do so.

15. Enter **InvCode** in the next field and set the field's Data Type to **Text**. Set Field Size to **7** and enter the Caption as **Inventory Code**. Set the Required property to **Yes**. Set the Indexed property to **Yes (Duplicates OK)**.

16. While holding down the **Control** key, select the **PONumber** and **InvCode** fields by clicking on their row selectors.

17. Click on the **Primary Key** icon. This will allow both fields to be the primary key.

18. Enter **POInvQuantity** in the next field name and set its Data Type to **Number**. Set the Field Size property to **Long Integer** and the Decimal Places property to **0**. Set the Caption property to **Quantity**.

19. Enter **InvCost** in the last field name and set its Data Type to **Currency**. Set the Caption property to **Cost**.

20. Save the table as **T Purchase Order Sub** and close.

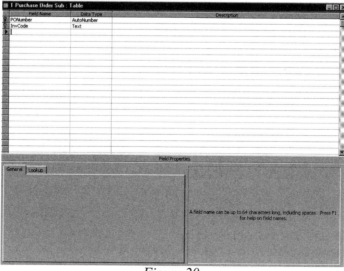

Figure 20

21. Click on the **Relationships** icon again. Choose the menu bar command **Relationships** - select **Show Table** from the pull-down menu. Add **T Inventory** and **T Purchase Order Sub**. Create a link between the two tables that is based on **InvCode**. Be sure to click the **Enforce Referential Integrity** check box. Save the new relationship and close the **Relationships** window.

22. Create a new form by clicking **Forms** and selecting the **New** icon in the **Database** window. Highlight **Form Wizard** and be sure that **T Purchase Order Sub** is selected in the **Tables/Queries** box.

23. Double-click on **POInvQuantity**, **InvCode**, and **InvCost**, respectively. Click on **Next**.

24. Select the **Tabular** format and then choose a style for the form. Delete the title text and click the radio button to allow you to modify the form's design. Next click on **Finish**.

25. Increase the size of the newly created form to 4 ½ to 5 inches.

26. Left align both the **Quantity** header and **Cost** header.

27. Choose the menu bar command **Edit** - **Select Form** (or click in the upper left-hand box just below the form's title bar where the two rulers meet), then choose the menu bar command **View** - **Properties** to open the property sheet for the form.

28. Select the **Record Source** property and click on the **Build** button (it has 3 dots on it). Click **Yes** to open the form's **Query Builder** window. The **Record Source** property specifies the source of the data for a form or a report. It can be a Table name, a Query name, or an SQL statement.

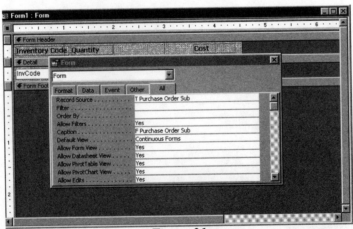

Figure 21

29. Choose the menu command **Query** – **Show Table** (or click) and add the **T Inventory** table. Close the **Show Table** window.

30. Click and drag the **PONumber** field from **T Purchase Order Sub** to the first field cell in the QBE grid, then set its Sort order to Ascending. See *Figure 22*.

31. Click and drag the **POInvQuantity** field from **T Purchase Order Sub** to the second field cell in the QBE grid. Click and drag the **InvCode** and the **InvCost** fields from **T Purchase Order Sub** to the third and fourth field cells, respectively.

32. Click and drag the **asterisk** row from **T Inventory** to the fifth field cell in the QBE grid. Note that **T Inventory*** appears in the cell. Selecting the **asterisk** captures all rows from that table.

Figure 22

33. Click **Run** ▓. Return to the design view by selecting **File - Close - Yes**. Close the **Properties** window.

34. Right click on the **InvCode** control box in the **Detail** section and select **Properties** from the pull-down menu. Make sure the **Control Source** property (**Data** tab) is set to **T Purchase Order Sub.InvCode**. If it is not, use the **Control Source** pull-down menu and select it. The **Control Source** property specifies what data is to appear in the control. As stated before, a control can be bound to a table, query, or SQL statement. It can also be the result of an expression (i.e., a combination of field names, controls, constants, functions, operators, etc.).

35. On the form, arrange all controls and their labels (e.g., **Quantity, Inventory Code**, and **Cost**) in a horizontal manner, leaving a space to insert **Description** between **Inventory Code** and **Cost**. Shrink the width of the control boxes for **Quantity** and **Cost**.

36. From the menu bar, click on the **View** pull-down menu to select the **Toolbox**. In the **Toolbox** window, click the **Text Box** ▓ tool and draw a new control in the **Detail** section of the form in between the controls for **Inventory Code** and **Cost**. Delete the textbox label associated with the new control. Click on the **Label** icon and draw a label in the **Form Header** section above the new control. Type "**Description**" in the new label box.

37. Right click on the **Description** control box and select **Properties** from the pull down menu. Click on the **Data** tab and set the **Control Source** property for the new text box to **InvDescription**

38. In the **Properties** window, for both **InvDescription** and **InvCost,** change the controls as follows:

- Click on the **Data** tab and change the **Enabled** property to **No**. The Enabled property specifies whether the field can receive user input.
- Click on the **Data** tab and change the **Locked** property to **Yes**. The Locked property specifies whether the field can be edited by the user in the Form view.

Note that setting these two properties in this fashion embeds internal controls in the database. This prevents unauthorized editing of the data.

- Click on the **Other** tab and change the **Tab Stop** property to **No**. The Tab Stop specifies whether the cursor will stop in a particular field when the tab or enter key is hit.
- Click on the **Format** tab and change the **Back Color** property to **12632256** (or choose gray from the color palette). The Back Color property specifies the color in the interior of a control box.
- Click on the **Format** tab and change the **Border Style** property to **Transparent**. The Border Style property specifies the type of border surrounding a control box.

Note that setting these three properties in this fashion facilitates form design. They signal to the user that no input is intended in these fields.

39. You will have to set the **Control Source (Data** tab) for **InvCost** so that the cost for each inventory item will appear. Think about where this data is stored.

40. Close and save the form as **F Purchase Order Sub**.

41. Create a new form using the **Form Wizard** for **T Purchase Order**. Include all of the fields in the form. Accept **Columnar** and select a style. Title the form **F Purchase Order**. Click the radio button that allows you to modify the form's design.

42. Use the mouse to create a sufficient amount of working room (both width and depth) in the form window.

43. Give the form a heading (e.g., **Purchase Order Form**) with similar size and font to headings included in the forms you created for suppliers and inventory.

44. From the **Toolbox** window, click on the **Subform/Subreport** ▦ icon. Draw the outline of a subform in the bottom area of the **Detail** section. Cancel the **Subform/Subreport Wizard**.

45. Delete the subform's label.

46. Right-click inside the new object, select **Properties** and select the **Source Object** property to **F Purchase Order Sub**. **PONumber** should automatically appear for **Link Child** and **Link Master** fields (**Data** tab). If not, use the pull-down menu to select it. Close the **Properties** window.

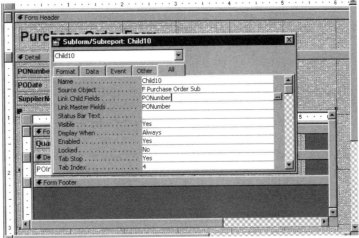

Figure 23

47. Select **Edit - Select Form** from the menu bar and then select the **Record Source** property (**Data** tab) and click on the **Build** button (it has 3 dots on it). Click **Yes** in the dialogue box that appears to open the form's **Query Builder** window.

48. Select **Query - Show Table** from the menu bar. Add **T Supplier** and close the **Show Table** window.

49. Click and drag the **PONumber** field from **T Purchase Order** to the first field cell in the QBE grid and then designate **Sort** as ascending.

50. Click and drag the remaining two fields from **T Purchase Order** to the second and third QBE grid field cells.

51. Click and drag the **SupplierName** field from the **T Supplier** to the fourth QBE grid field cell. Now, select **Query - Run** ▮. Save and close the query to return to the form in the **Design View**. Close the form **Properties** window.

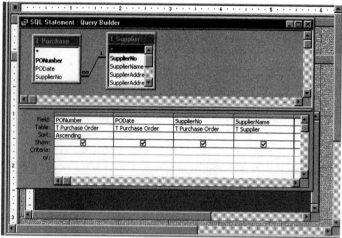

Figure 24

52. Use the **Text Box** tool in the **Toolbox** window to create a new control just to the right of the **Supplier Number** control. Delete the new control's label. Set the **Control Source** property (**Data** tab) to **SupplierName**. Set the **Enabled** property (**Data** tab) to **No**, the **Locked** property (**Data** tab) to **Yes**, and the **Tab Stop** property (**Other** tab) to **No**. Set the **Font Size** (**Format** tab) to 10 and make the **Font Weight** property (**Format** tab) to bold. Set the **Back Color** property (**Format** tab) to **12632256**, and the **Border Style** property (**Format** tab) to **Transparent**. Close the **Properties** window and save the form as **F Purchase Order**.

53. Open the **Purchase Order** form and create Purchase Order No. 9682 for the following transaction:

> On December 16, 2003, Franz Bieler (CA Buyer) ordered 18,000 lbs. of white grapes (inventory code: WG20004) at $1.05 per pound from Mendocino Vineyards (Supplier #: P0652).

54. If you wish to quit *Access* at this time, simply close the program and your database will be saved with the name you used to create it.

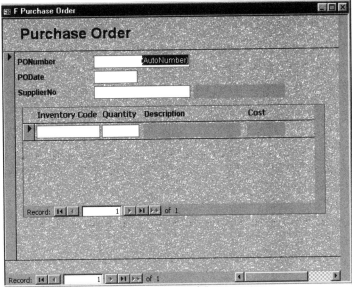

Figure 25

CREATING A QUERY

Recall that queries can be used to ask questions about data or to perform actions on data. As you will now see, they can also be used as the basis for a report. You will need to create a purchase order to send to the supplier to order the inventory required by Chateau Americana. To do this, you will have to build a query that will obtain data from fields in several different tables. In this query, you will create a field that will calculate totals by extending unit prices and quantities ordered and a field that combines several address fields into a single address field.

Requirements
1. Open *Access* database you created and dick on the **Queries** tab in the **Database** window, click on the **New** button, then, with **Design View** highlighted in the **New Query** dialogue box, click the **OK** button.

2. Highlight all four previously created tables (T Inventory, T Purchase Order, T Purchase Order Sub, and T Supplier) by clicking on each while holding down the **Shift** key, and click on **Add**. Close the **Show Table** window.

3. Drag and click the fields from the tables listed below to the QBE grid Field cells:

   T Purchase Order fields:
   - **PONumber**
   - **PODate**
   - **SupplierNo**

T Inventory fields:
- **InvCode**
- **InvDescription**
- **InvCost**

T Supplier fields:
- **SupplierName**
- **SupplierAddress1**
- **SupplierAddress2**
- **SupplierCity**
- **SupplierState**
- **SupplierZip**

T Purchase Order Sub field:
- **POInvQuantity**

4. Set the QBE grid **Sort** cells for **PONumber** and **InvCode** from **T Purchase Order** and **InvCode** from **T Inventory** to **Ascending**.

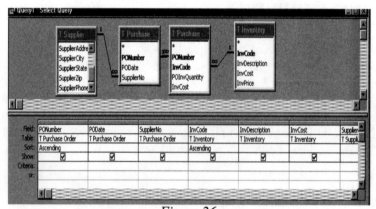

Figure 26

5. It is necessary to concatenate (i.e., link together) the city, state, and zip code fields. This is done by creating an additional field in the next open Field cell in the QBE grid. Click on the next open Field cell and then click on the **Build** icon to bring up the **Expression Builder** window. In the lower left portion of the **Expression Builder** window, double-click on the + symbol next to **Tables** and click on **T Supplier**.

IMPORTANT NOTE: In the following instructions, the symbol ^ represents a space.

6. In the upper portion of the **Expression Builder** window, type **SupplierAddressComp:^**

7. In the middle lower portion of the Expression Builder window, double-click on **SupplierCity**. Notice that when you did this the field name appeared in the upper portion of the window **BUT** some unwanted text also appeared that you will need to remove. Before you do, let's finish the expression.

8. Type **& ", ^" &** (with quotation marks) then double-click on **SupplierState**, type **& " ^^ " &** (with quotation marks) and double-click on **SupplierZip**. Now we will go back and remove the unwanted text. Scroll back to the beginning of the field name. Note that when you double-clicked on **SupplierCity**, *Access* inserted "«Expr»" into the expression just after the field name **SupplierAddressComp**. This must be deleted for the expression to work. Next click **OK**.

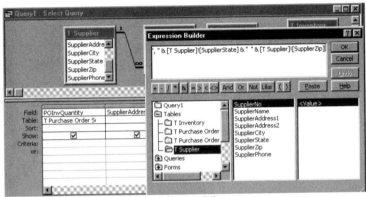

Figure 27

9. The next open QBE grid Field cell will be used to calculate the extension for the cost times the quantity ordered. The Build button can again be utilized to obtain help in entering the text for this field. Enter **Extension: [T Purchase Order Sub]![POInvQuantity]*[T Inventory]![InvCost]**. Next click **OK**.

10. Click on the **Run** button to test the query. The result should include each of the fields listed above as well as the two new fields created in steps 6 through 9. Close and save this query as **Q Purchase Order**.

11. If you wish to quit *Access* at this time, simply close the program and your database will be saved with the name you used to create it.

CREATING A REPORT

The purchase order form you have created is an internal form. Its intent was to provide a convenient, user-friendly form for employees, but it is not in a format that provides all the information needed by suppliers. Therefore, it will be necessary to create a **report** (using *Access* terminology) that can be sent to suppliers when Chateau Americana wants to make a purchase. You will use the query that you just created to build this report.

Requirements

1. Open your *Access* database and dick on the **Report** tab in the **Database** window, click on the **New** button, select **Design View**, and select **Q Purchase Order** from the pull down menu. Then click **OK**.

2. Click and drag the right edge of the report to about the 6-inch mark on the top ruler. Click and drag the **Page Footer** and **Page Header** area edges up to reduce the height of each to zero. **NOTE: You will not enter anything into these sections!!!**

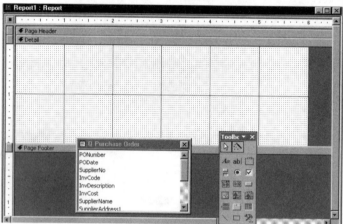

Figure 28

3. Click on the **Sorting and Grouping** icon from the menu bar and enter **PONumber** in the first Field/Expression cell in the **Sorting and Grouping** dialogue box. Click on the **Group Header** in the **Properties** window and change the property to **Yes**. Do the same for the **Group Footer**. Set the **Keep Together** property to **Whole Group**, then press **Alt-F4** to close the dialogue box.

4. Click on the **Field List** toolbar button from the main menu, then click and drag the following fields to the **Detail** section.

   - **InvCode**
   - **InvDescription**
   - **InvCost**
   - **POInvQuantity**
   - **Extension**

   Each field will become a control on the report. Close the **Field List** window.

5. Click on the **Inventory Code** label (**NOT** the control box, just the label) and press Ctrl-X. This will cut the label away from the control box. Click on the **PONumber Header** bar, then press Ctrl-V to place the label in that section. Do the same for the remaining labels. Line the labels up horizontally with the control boxes just below their related labels.

6. Enlarge the **Header** section by dragging the **Detail** bar downward. Bring down the labels for the **Detail** section also.

Figure 29

7. Using the **Field List** again, click and drag the following fields to the PONumber Header section:

   - **PONumber**
   - **PODate**
   - **SupplierNo**
   - **SupplierName**
   - **SupplierAddress1**
   - **SupplierAddress2**
   - **SupplierAddressComp**

   Delete the labels for everything but the purchase order number. Arrange the control boxes using good form design principles. Close the **Field List** window.

8. Using the **Label** icon from the **Toolbox** window, create a label for Chateau Americana's name, address and telephone number at the top of the purchase order. Use an appropriate font size so that the supplier will know immediately who the buyer is.

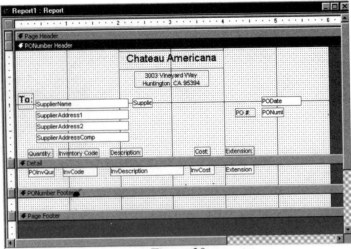

Figure 30

9. A **Control** box must be made to calculate the total of the extension amounts for each line of the purchase order. Use the **Text Box** tool from the **Toolbox** window to create a control in the **PONumber** footer section. Position the control box just below the **Extension** control box in the **Detail** section. Set its **Control Source** property to =**Sum([Extension])** and its **Format** property to **Currency**. Set the attached label **Caption** property to **Total**.

10. Look at the report you have just created by clicking on the **Print Preview** icon from the menu bar. Feel free to change the formatting (e.g., font sizes, bold, etc.) for any field you desire. The key is to utilize good form design principles to enhance the user's understanding of the purchase order.

11. Close and save the report as **R Purchase Order**.

12. You have now completed the *Access* assignment. Simply close the program and your database will be saved with the name you used to create it.

SUMMARY

In the preceding exercises, you have explored some of the power behind a database management system. You have created *Access* tables. You have learned the importance of primary keys and foreign keys. You have created queries to create composite fields and to combine fields from multiple tables into a single form or report. You have designed forms to display the information in a more user-friendly, intuitive manner and you have entered the data into those forms to see how they work. Finally, you have designed a report using the data from multiple tables. But this is just the beginning. There is much more to learn about database systems!